WE THE
UNICORNS

ONLY TRUE

YouTube

FANS will complete

THIS → QUIZ

BOOK

So you think you're a YouTube guru?
Well, this book will show you how all-knowing you really are! If you flunk out, use this book to sharpen your YouTube knowledge – before anyone notices you might not be a true fan.

There are quizzes on everything you love about YouTube and your favourite YouTubers. Take a quiz to see what your channel should be about and if you'd make it as a daily vlogger. Or test your knowledge of YouTuber's birthdays, middle names and much more. There are some tough questions and some downright random ones – you've got to answer them all. Whether you love beauty, gaming or daily vlogs, test your true YouTube fan status here.

Wherever you see the True YouTube Fan button, turn to **page 137** and add your score.

Once you've completed this *ENTIRE* book, you'll be able to find out your true fan status.

Good luck, YouTube fans!

We Regret To Inform You That This Quiz Is Indeed, The

Hardest

Let's throw you straight in at the deep end. Time to prove that you've got what it takes to fangirl your way to the top of the screaming mess of YouTube fans! Simply answer all 15 questions and then check your answers at the back of the book. If you fail, you might as well give up now – or at least sit through 20 hours of YouTube.

Bad news: you won't pass this quiz.

TRUE
YOUTUBE
FAN!

1 Manny Mua became the first male star of which makeup brand?

a) **Maybelline**
b) **CoverGirl**
c) **Barry M**

2 Which YouTuber was on GQ's 2017 'Best Dressed Men' list?

a) **Jack Harries**
b) **Jim Chapman**
c) **Alfie Deyes**

3 What did Dan Howell make out of iron beads on New Year's Eve 2016?

a) **Rapidash**
b) **Pikachu**
c) **Snorlax**

4 Which High School Musical member reunited with Ashley Tisdale on their YouTube channel for a new song?

a) **Zac Efron**
b) **Corbin Bleu**
c) **Vanessa Hudgens**

5 What's the name of the YouTube channel that threatened to 'dethrone PewDiePie'?

a) **LittleBabyBum**
b) **Fun Toys Collector Disney Toys Review**
c) **Ryan ToysReview**

6 Who won the Teen Choice Award for 'Favourite YouTube Star' in January 2016?

a) **JennaMarbles**
b) **Connor Franta**
c) **Tyler Oakley**

7 Which YouTuber released The Luxe Life book?

a) **Patricia Bright**
b) **bubzbeauty**
c) **Fleur DeForce**

8 What is John Green's middle name?

a) **Christopher**
b) **Michael**
c) **Hank**

9 Who became the first female UK YouTuber to get a diamond play button?

a) **Zoë Sugg**
b) **Dodie Clark**
c) **Carrie Hope Fletcher**

10 Which country finally made YouTube legal in 2016?

a) **America**
b) **Iraq**
c) **Pakistan**

11 Which one of these magazines did Zoella appear on the cover of?

a) **Cosmopolitan**
b) **Time**
c) **Diva**

12 Dan Howell once had a hamster, what was its name?

a) **Penny**
b) **Leila**
c) **Suki**

13 What did Lilly Singh study at university?

a) **Psychology**
b) **Philosophy**
c) **Physical Education**

14 What is the most covered song on YouTube?

a) **'Hello' by Adele**
b) **'Baby One More Time' by Britney Spears**
c) **'All of Me' by John Legend**

15 Who made her dog fly?

a) **JennaMarbles**
b) **Tanya Burr**
c) **Zoë Sugg**

TRUE YOUTUBE FAN! ___ / **15**

Turn to page **139** for the answers

Results!

0–5: You were warned that this was the hardest quiz ever. You weren't listening. You have a long way to go to prove that you're a true YouTube fan.

6–10: Why did you bother taking this quiz?! You knew it was the hardest. You need to broaden your channel subscriptions.

11–14: Not bad, even though you were warned it was the hardest trivia quiz ever. Next time go for gold and full marks for the ultimate prestige.

15: Actually, you did good considering this really is the hardest quiz ever. Go straight to page 137 and enter this award-winning score, then bask in your own glory!

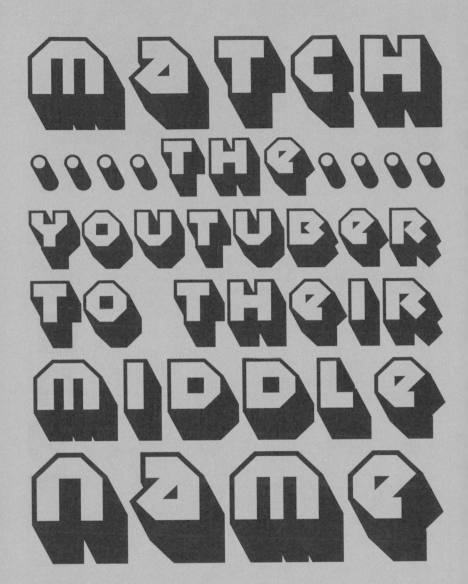

MATCH .....THE..... YOUTUBER TO THEIR MIDDLE NAME

Have you ever had a weird urge to find out the middle name of every single YouTuber? Simply match the middle names at the top of the next page to the YouTubers below. Take your time and think carefully, because the score from this quiz will totally affect your overall true fan score. Good luck!

Elizabeth **Joel** **James**

Arvid Ulf **Miranda** **Michael**

Nicole **Mae** **Andrew**

 Dodie _____ Clark

 Jenna _____ Mourey

 Phillip _____ DeFranco

 Connor _____ Franta

 Phil _____ Lester

 Colleen _____ Ballinger

 Zoë _____ Sugg

 Ian _____ Hecox

 Felix _____ Kjellberg

 ___ / 9

Turn to page **139** for the answers

FIND OUT WHICH

YOUTUBE

FRIENDSHIP

GROUP YOU
BELONG
IN BASED
ON YOUR

FOOD

CHOICES

YouTube friendship groups are pretty special, TBH. Whether they met through meet-ups, their network or just a mutual love of each other's talent, there's no doubt you'd love to hang out with your favourite 'Tubers for the day. So to (kinda) help this come true, here's a quiz which will work out which YouTuber friendship group you belong in and it's all based on your food choices. Yum!

How do you like your sausages?

a) With mash and gravy

b) As battered as they come

c) Vegetarian/vegan friendly

d) In a sandwich

e) As German as possible

f) Chorizo style, please

Should pineapple be on pizza?

a) NO WAY!

b) On every kind

c) Not unless you're crazy

d) YES!

e) It has its time and place

f) I can't believe you even consider it as an option

Pick a condiment.

a) Ketchup

b) Mayo

c) Brown sauce

d) Hot sauce

e) Mustard

f) Tartar sauce

Which one of these has got to go?

a) Tacos

b) Coffee

c) Fried chicken

d) Cake

e) Chocolate

f) Fries

You can only eat one of these for breakfast. What do you pick?

a) Fruit Loops

b) Toast soaked in butter

c) Porridge

d) Pancakes

e) A plate of hash browns

f) Avocado on toast

Mostly As: The Kids Are Alright! You're fun and playful and never want to grow up. Hanging with the likes of Jacob Sartorius and Matty B would be a literal hoot. / Mostly Bs: The Zalfie Tribe. You belong with Zoe, Sean, Alfie, Poppy and Mark. Whether you'd be chilling in a treehouse or watching Christmas movies in July, you'd fit right in with this lot. / Mostly Cs: The Savage Squad. You're fierce, bold, ambitious and you love empowering the people around you. You need a friendship group who are going to help you become the true queen you really are. / Mostly Ds: The American Girls: Lilly Singh, iJustine, Cassey Ho, Rosana Pansino and Lindsay Stirling are the all-American dream and you totally belong in their friendship group. / Mostly Es: Revelmoders. Your perfect night out is having a gaming tournament or hitting up a cool gig and you're never always the life and soul of any party! / Mostly Fs: The YouTube Boyband. You're musically talented, a bit kooky and will do anything for a laugh. You'd happily hang out with the YouTube boyband if it meant getting up to mischief.

11

Can You Meet Your Favourite YouTuber And Stay Cool?

This next quiz will take you – quite literally – through the entire book, because it's an epic storytelling challenge; and all you have to do is decide which pages to turn to. You might say you're going on an adventure of your own choosing.

Here's how it works:

- Read the scenario below, and the options for what to do next.
- Pick an option and turn to the corresponding page.
- Repeat as necessary until you reach the end.
- Congrats! You've built a whole story.

In this story, you'll be playing the role of a YouTuber fan – difficult, we know. You're going to one of the biggest annual YouTube meet-up events in the world; but can you successfully meet your favourite creator AND keep your cool? It's harder than it sounds...

1: START

The only way to get into the meet and greets at the event is to get a separate ticket – and you're one of thousands of fans waiting online for them to go on sale. But you're starting to feel a bit hungry...

- To quickly make a snack, turn to page **20**
- To sit and wait for tickets to go live, turn to page **32**

AQ:

Look out for the adventure quiz boxes throughout the book. There are two adventures, one starting here and the other on page 102. Good luck, and don't mess it up!

Name The YouTuber From The Picture Clues

This is a deceptively simple but deviously hard little puzzle. The usernames of nine popular YouTubers have been translated into picture clues. Your task is to work out which YouTuber the picture clues are describing – easy, right? It's harder than you think. Check out the example below before you get going:

PewDiePie

1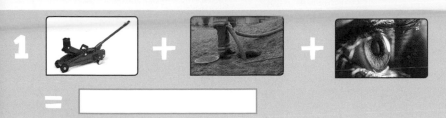

= [_____]

2

= [_____]

3

= [_____]

4

= [_____]

5

= [_____]

6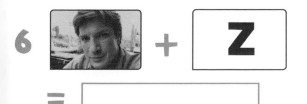

= [_____]

TRUE YOUTUBE FAN! ___ / 6

Turn to page **139** for the answers

WHAT KIND OF PERSON WOULD YOU BE IN THE SIMS?

The best thing about playing The Sims is the fact that you can be whoever you want to be without reality getting in the way. So, whether you're playing it to have your dream job, or purely to mess with the neighbourhood Sims, everyone has a particular play style. Over the next five questions you'll be subjected to a very scientific method of psychoanalysis to determine your result. Answer as truthfully as possible and you'll discover your inner truth – because there's a deep, dark Sim hidden inside all of us.

AQ: You decided to wear one of the t-shirts you bought from the YouTuber's merch store – but oh no! When you get to the line at the event, there are dozens of people wearing the same thing. How will you stand out from the crowd to your idol?

- To do something crazy in your photo op, turn to page 66
- To scream and catch their attention from the line, turn to page 84

1 Okay, so why are you playing The Sims in the first place?

a) **Fantasising about real life**
b) **The challenge of 'winning' the game**
c) **I just like torturing Sims**
d) **Escapism, basically**

2 In your honest opinion, who would be the WORST YouTuber to play The Sims?

a) **iDubbbzTV**
b) **JennaMarbles**
c) **CrankGameplays**
d) **Lilly Singh**

3 Be honest, which YouTuber are you most likely to remake and marry in The Sims?

a) **Markiplier**
b) **Zoella**
c) **Miranda Sings**
d) **Connor Franta**

4 For real, which YouTuber would probably die first in The Sims?

a) **Tana Mongeau**
b) **jacksepticeye**
c) **Louise Pentland**
d) **Shane Dawson**

5 Lastly, pick an emoji that summarises you the most.

a) 🖤
b) 💰
c) 💀
d) 😊

Mostly As: You'd have LOTS of relationships with the locals, and possibly multiple children... carpe diem! / Mostly Bs: You'd be that person who actually put cheats into the game, lived like a God for three days and then got bored. / Mostly Cs: You'd make families just to kill them off and hang out with the Grim Reaper. / Mostly Ds: Honestly, you'd have the best life ever in The Sims. You'd have your dream job, dream family and extra cash in the bank.

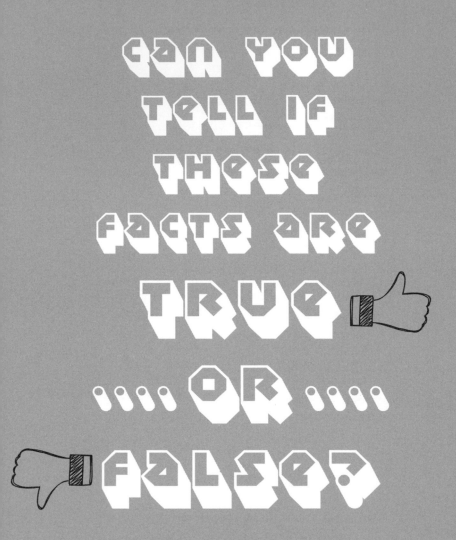

CAN YOU TELL IF THESE FACTS ARE TRUE OR FALSE?

Real or No real is basically a version of true or false and here's a brand spanking new YouTube version of it. The game is simple: on the quiz page there are a bunch of facts about 10 different YouTubers and all you have to do is work out if they're Real or No real.

And don't forget to fill in your True YouTube Fan scoresheet after you've checked how many you got right — no cheating!

1 Phil Lester was once an extra in British soap Emmerdale. Real ☐ No real ☐

2 Tanya Burr used to work as a makeup artist on a Benefit cosmetics counter.
Real ☐ No real ☐

3 Joe Sugg was rejected to appear as an extra in Harry Potter because he was too short.
Real ☐ No real ☐

4 Marcus Butler is shipped with his colleague Matt and people call them Mattcus.
Real ☐ No real ☐

5 Mark Ferris has been in an Ellie Goulding music video. Real ☐ No real ☐

6 Zoë Sugg's middle name is Victoria.
Real ☐ No real ☐

7 PewDiePie once had a trial for Manchester United Under 21s football team.
Real ☐ No real ☐

8 Connor Franta's mum is called Diane.
Real ☐ No real ☐

9 Anna Saccone met Jonathan Joly when he cast her in a music video that he was directing. Real ☐ No real ☐

10 Dan Howell had a dog named Suki.
Real ☐ No real ☐

TRUE YOUTUBE FAN!

___ / 10

Turn to page **139** for the answers

How Well Do You Remember The Lyrics To Dan's Diss Track?

This is literally going to be the easiest quiz in the whole world. It looks like the entire YouTube community is obsessed with Dan's roast track and his fire lyrics. So, here are 12 questions to test your knowledge on Dan's diss track. From Winnie The Pooh to veganism, can you remember the lyrics to one of the most iconic rap songs of 2016?

AQ: You made yourself a lil' something to eat — and nice, you're back in time. Better yet, you managed to get tickets in the ballot! Now, to plan your outfit for meeting your fave...

- To wear some of their merch, turn to page 16
- To wear something cool, turn to page 34

1 What video does Dan make after he comes back from a month of not uploading?

a) **A challenge**
b) **A tag**
c) **A clothing haul**

2 What's the best way to drag a Dan Howell?

a) **By his fringe**
b) **By the ear**
c) **By his walk**

3 In what year was Dan's hair cool?

a) **2008**
b) **1752**
c) **2007**

4 Who would you need to breed with Winnie The Pooh to create a Dan Howell?

a) **Slenderman**
b) **Spider-Man**
c) **Tigger**

5 Why does Dan procrastinate making videos?

a) **It's boring**
b) **Being judged is scary**
c) **He's too busy playing Pokémon Go**

6 What does Dan do too much of?

a) **Sleeping**
b) **Gaming**
c) **Eating**

ZZZz

7 How long was Dan a vegan for?

a) **Three days**
b) **Three weeks**
c) **Three hours**

MORE QUESTIONS THIS WAY

8 Why do people ship Dan with Phil?
- **a)** It's funny
- **b)** It's kawaii
- **c)** It's problematic

9 What did Tumblr call Dan problematic for making?
- **a)** Fan fiction
- **b)** Toast
- **c)** Dil Howlter

10 Who is Dan's new celebrity crush?
- **a)** Jennifer Lawrence
- **b)** Phil Lester
- **c)** Evan Peters

11 What sexuality is Dan secretly trying to repress?
- **a)** Bisexual
- **b)** Asexual
- **c)** Furry

12 Which one YouTuber got a shoutout in Dan's diss track?
- **a)** JennaMarbles
- **b)** Ryan Higa
- **c)** Phil Lester

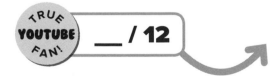

TRUE YOUTUBE FAN! ___ / 12

Turn to page **139** for the answers

Find Your Fave

It's mystic puzzle time. This word search has been enchanted with black magic and YouTube dust in order to give it magical prediction powers. Possibly. Maybe. Who knows? Here's how it works: the first name you see will be the name of your favourite YouTuber – and the second name you see is the YouTuber you should collaborate with. It's time to see if your eyes are truly guided by your heart.

```
I  K  I  P  N  N  H  X  S  F  O  F  N  I  N  W  T  N  C  G
I  I  N  F  A  T  R  L  U  X  Q  G  N  Y  K  X  A  H  W  C
D  L  V  K  T  G  M  A  R  K  I  P  L  I  E  R  A  P  S  E
Q  Z  L  K  H  C  Q  X  H  E  O  D  P  M  T  V  J  D  H  I
Z  F  Q  J  A  C  K  S  E  P  T  I  C  E  Y  E  Y  O  B  P
E  J  E  O  N  Q  M  R  V  H  M  Q  B  A  U  S  A  K  E  E
O  Z  W  E  Z  A  L  H  R  I  X  G  Z  L  W  B  T  Z  A  F
C  J  I  Y  E  P  G  R  I  L  T  W  K  F  P  C  O  R  J  N
W  T  F  G  D  E  A  B  Y  I  R  A  M  I  S  B  U  X  Q  U
P  I  V  R  T  I  U  Q  I  P  O  H  R  E  Q  O  N  T  I  Q
H  L  H  A  X  E  V  D  A  D  Y  R  H  D  T  X  I  Y  J  O
I  T  F  C  H  A  P  A  F  E  E  G  L  E  G  Y  S  D  F  L
L  H  F  E  B  S  E  N  X  J  S  J  W  Y  Z  C  W  O  D  V
L  Y  L  F  A  P  W  H  A  R  I  A  S  E  V  G  T  S  A  T
E  F  H  F  Q  E  O  O  N  A  V  B  C  S  Y  Q  E  S  B  T
S  R  L  A  E  P  N  W  G  N  A  O  Q  U  Z  M  F  S  Q  N
T  A  E  E  I  O  T  E  T  C  N  C  V  G  V  C  U  X  P  W
E  N  F  R  Y  Z  V  L  M  O  N  P  D  I  Q  B  H  V  H  X
R  K  Q  V  S  Z  H  L  B  B  S  A  S  S  Y  A  Q  V  H  X
B  W  S  Y  L  O  U  I  S  E  P  E  N  T  L  A  N  D  M  F
```

_____ is my favourite YouTuber.

I should collaborate with _____.

23

CAN YOU PLAN A YOUTUBER EVENT WITHOUT GOING OVER BUDGET?

VidCon, Playlist Live, Summer In The City and now Hello World – all epic YouTube events that reach thousands of people across the globe. But there's about to be a new event in town, or at least there will be if you can manage to stay within your budget.

The way this quiz works is simple, you've got a YouTube event to plan and £150,000 to do it with. Through a series of choices, you'll find out whether you'd go bust, stay on track and hold an awesome event or way underspend and leave fans disappointed. No pressure then, right?

1 You come up with a brilliant idea to plan a YouTube event but where are you going to host it?

a) **Great Exuma**

b) **London**

c) **Birmingham**

d) **Brighton**

e) **LA**

f) **New York**

2 How many days is your event going to last?

a) **Just the one**

b) **Two to three days**

c) **An entire week**

3 You need a headline act for the event, which one of these creators would you book?

a) **Zoë Sugg**

b) **Tyler Oakley**

c) **Miles McKenna**

d) **Lucy & Lydia**

e) **Mark Ferris**

f) **Patricia Bright**

4 And you absolutely need a music act, who do you go for?

a) **Dodie Clark**

b) **Lucy Moon**

c) **Emma Blackery**

d) **Matty B**

e) **Troye Sivan**

f) **Pentatonix**

5 Pick another creator to book for your event.

a) **Grace Victory**

b) **Just Jodes**

c) **Rose and Rosie**

d) **Oli White**

e) **Louise Pentland**

f) **The Lean Machines**

6

Pick an added extra.

a) **Free pick 'n' mix**
b) **Waltzers**
c) **Industry talks**
d) **A photo booth**
e) **A YouTuber book library**
f) **Goodie bags**

7

How are you organising the meet and greets?

a) **There are none**
b) **A raffle ticket style ballot**
c) **First come, first served**

8

What merch are you selling?

a) **Just YouTubers' merch**
b) **Posters and t-shirts with my event logo**
c) **EVERYTHING – hoodies, keychains, mugs, dog leads...**

9

How much are you charging for tickets?

a) **It's free**
b) **£20-£50 per day**
c) **£100 + extra for meet and greets**

10

Finally, pick a creator to attend.

a) **Amelia Liana**

b) **Ace Trainer Liam**

c) **Scola Dondo**

d) **Grace Helbig**

e) **Alfie Deyes**

f) **Ricky Dillon**

RESULTS THIS WAY →

Use this nifty score sheet to add up your answers.

	A	B	C	D	E	F	Score:
1	+3	+2	+1	+1	+2	+3	
2	+1	+2	+3				
3	+3	+3	+2	+1	+1	+2	
4	+2	+1	+2	+1	+3	+3	
5	+1	+1	+2	+3	+3	+2	
6	+3	+2	+1	+2	+1	+3	
7	+1	+2	+3				
8	+1	+2	+3				
9	+3	+2	+1				
10	+2	+1	+1	+3	+3	+2	

10 – 15
You spent £100,100
You're WAY under budget – go add a few more YouTubers to the line up and chuck in a bunch more merchandise stands. Your event needs to be big if it's going to be a success.

16 – 25
You spent £149,997
You're bang on the money (with a few quid left over for a frappe to celebrate). Your event is going to be the only thing people are talking about for literally years. You've got a solid mix of household name creators and a few newbies too. The event is packed with fun extras and you haven't been too greedy when it comes to milking people for their dollar. Well done, you!

26+
You spent £900,000
You've gone WAY over budget and, as a result, the event is having to be cancelled because you've gone bankrupt. There are a lot of angry parents and YouTube fans out there right now. Our suggestion is to lie low and maybe never plan anything ever again.

UNSCRAMBLE

THESE YOUTUBER NAMES IN THE ULTIMATE ANAGRAM QUIZ

TRUE YOUTUBE FAN! __ / 14

Turn to page **139** for the answers

Alright folks, this one will take some brainpower and some obsessive knowledge of YouTubers. Luckily, if you're reading this book then it means you almost certainly have both. The quiz page is filled with some pretty devious anagrams and your task is to work out which anagram is which YouTuber's name. Make sure you hurry, 'cos the fate of the world is at stake, probably. Let's pretend it is, as that will add a nice layer of danger. Best of luck – or as they say in anagram town 'buckle soft'.

1. ZEAL LO

She is known for her haul videos and has a sibling who is also a YouTuber.

2. ACE STICKY JEEP

This lad is known for gaming, screaming and screaming while gaming.

3. CARDED KILO

She smells like lemongrass and sleep...

4. HELPER LIST

Known as the inventor of a popular time-based game and app.

5. EASILY FEED

We could tell you who this is, but that would render the whole quiz pointless.

6. A KEY TROLLEY

The next Ellen.

7. LYING HILLS

Don't let the word 'lying' in the anagram fool you, this YouTuber is actually very nice – and something of a boss.

8. REPAIR MILK

A voice even smoother than milk.

9. HANDSAWS ONE

Used to have an emo fringe (didn't we all?) but no longer.

10. HAZY KILOS

This YouTuber has more energy than several combined suns.

11. HAG RAINY

The original top dog.

12. JAMS FLICKS

Him him, he a big boy.

13. JOY CANS CLOSE

Top of the morning to all one million of them.

14. WELLHEAD LION

Loves to be referred to by his old username.

MATCH THE YOUTUBER TO THE TREND THEY INVENTED

YouTubers are more than just creative, they're also inventive. Here are some of the awesome trends and games invented by YouTubers and your job is to see just how many you can match to their creator.

WHICH YOUTUBER INVENTED THE...

1. First Time Tag

2. Roast Yourself Challenge

3. Harlem Shake (YouTube trend)

4. 7 Second Challenge

5. Boyfriend Does My Voiceover Challenge

6. 100 Layers Of... Trend

FILTHY FRANK

SIMPLY NAILOGICAL

LOUISE PENTLAND

RYAN HIGA

KEEPINGUPWITHXK

PHIL LESTER

TRUE YOUTUBE FAN!

_____ / 6

Turn to page **139** for the answers

TEST YOUR PARENTS' YOUTUBE KNOWLEDGE

Just how much YouTube knowledge has your parent or guardian absorbed by being around you? How well do they know their YouTubers? It's time to find out with this handy-dandy quiz – don't worry, it isn't *too* hard!

Don't panic this doesn't count towards your True YouTube Fan scoresheet – it's for you to score and judge them.

AQ: You decide to wait – but even when the tickets finally go live, you still aren't one of the lucky ones! What's the point of even going to the event if you can't meet your fave?

- To stay at home, turn to page 60
- To go to the event anyway, turn to page 50

1. WHICH ONE IS DAN?

2. WHAT IS THE NAME OF THIS WOMAN'S YOUTUBE PERSONA?

a) Zola
b) Zoella
c) Zobelle

3. HOW MANY YOUTUBE USERS ARE THERE?

a) Between one million and one hundred million
b) Between 500 million and a billion
c) Over a billion

4. WHICH OF THESE YOUTUBERS HAS THE MOST SUBSCRIBERS?

a) PewDiePie
b) Zoella
c) Markiplier

5. WHAT IS 'SUMMER IN THE CITY'?

a) A popular YouTube series
b) A YouTube convention
c) A merchandise company

6. WHAT IS THIS GUY'S NAME?

a) Chris
b) Tim
c) Joe

7. WHAT NATIONALITY IS THIS GUY?

a) Irish
b) American
c) German

I'm sure you don't need the answers, but if you do (unacceptable!) turn to page 140.

Is This Connor Franta Or A Can Of Fanta?

This is POP culture!

Ever wondered if you could tell the difference between Connor Franta or a can of Fanta? Now's the time to test your wits and wile and bump up your scoresheet points! These are basically free points right here.

AQ:

You decided to wear your lucky 'first date' outfit, which all your friends will recognise in your photo with your YouTube fave later. You wonder if this would be a funny thing to tell them...

- To confess this secret to your YouTube fave, turn to page 88
- To say nothing, turn to page 40

1. Who is this?

a) Connor Franta
b) A can of Fanta

2. And who is this?

a) That's YouTuber Connor Franta
b) That's a can of Fanta

3. Who is this?

a) A can of Fanta
b) Connor Franta
c) Connor Fanta

4. And who is this?

a) Connor Franta
b) A can of Fanta
c) The great city of Atlanta

5. And this?

a) A can of Fanta
b) A noble manta
c) Connor Franta

6. What about this?

a) A can of Franta
b) Connor Franta
c) A can of Fanta

TRUE YOUTUBE FAN!

___ / 6

Turn to page **140** for the answers

Can You Guess The YouTuber From Their Birthday?

'I don't fancy doing much for my birthday this year,' said NO YOUTUBER EVER. From trending on Twitter to vlogs showing epic birthday celebrations, it seems as if you're sending birthday wishes to another big-name creator every day. And do they ever wish *you* happy birthday? No! You know, a card would have been enough... *sigh*

Anyway, how much attention have you been paying to your favourite YouTubers' birthdays? It's time to find out. Don't worry, there are a few little hints and clues along the way to help you out.

1 Which YouTuber celebrates their birthday on 1st June? Hint: She's known for her love of cats.

a) Gabriella Lindley
b) JennaMarbles
c) Ingrid Nilsen
d) GloZell Green

2 Which American YouTuber turned fashion designer was born on 7th November?

a) Liza Koshy
b) Colleen Ballinger
c) Amanda Cerny
d) Bethany Mota

3 This LGBTQ+ icon is a YouTube OG. They were born on 22nd March 1989. Who is it?

a) Hannah Hart
b) Tyler Oakley
c) Gigi Gorgeous
d) Kingsley

4 STORYTIME: This YouTuber was born on 24th June and has gone through more drama than most of us ever will.

a) Tana Mongeau
b) Louise Pentland
c) Roxxsaurus
d) The Gabbie Show

5 Which gaming YouTuber celebrates their birthday on 8th November? Clue: His birthday is sadly at the start of the month and not in the middle and this was a terrible joke.

a) jacksepticeye
b) PewDiePie
c) Markiplier
d) DanTDM

6 Which creator celebrates their birthday on 26th January, which is exactly one month after Boxing Day. Fact.

a) Oli White
b) KathleenLights
c) Patricia Bright
d) FernandoFight (we don't know who this is either, we made it up because it rhymed)

7 Part of a duo that pioneered the YouTube beauty community to real new heights, who has their birthday on the 23rd August?

a) Samantha Chapman
b) Niki Albon
c) Manny Mua
d) Zoë Sugg

TRUE YOUTUBE FAN! ___ /7

Turn to page **140** for the answers

Could You REALLY Make A Great YouTube Video?

Everybody thinks vlogging is a piece of cake – but do you REALLY know what it takes to make your videos great? Every boring thought-piece on YouTubers talks about how little they do in order to gain the following and success they've achieved. But you and I know that's not the case; or at least hopefully you do. It's time to find out!

1 How much time do you think goes into making one vlog?

a) **About a day's work**
b) **Depends, but at least a few hours**
c) **Literally a whole week**

2 What's the most important thing to consider before filming?

a) **The sound quality**
b) **The jump cuts**
c) **The pretty backdrop**

3 What does your video script look like?

a) **I have a general overview but there's room to improvise**
b) **I've written every single thing I'm going to say, even the jokes**
c) **Uhhh, script?**

4 Okay, you're done filming. How much editing will you need to do?

a) **Audio synching, compressing, colour correction, rendering...**
b) **Just cutting out the long pauses**
c) **How do I put text on it?**

5 Where do you get your background music?

a) **I asked someone for permission to use their music**
b) **YouTube's Audio Library always has something I need**
c) **I grab something I like from iTunes**

6 How did you caption your video?

a) **I paid for a captioning service**
b) **By hand**
c) **I don't need to!**

7 Your video is up! How are you going to share it?

a) **Daily reminders on every social network until my next video**
b) **I'll Tweet it out once, my followers will see that**
c) **My subscribers will see it in their feed**

Mostly As: Vlogging Pro! Well done! You've learned that there's a lot more work to vlogging than people realise; but you're doing it every single time you upload. You'll have your Gold Play Button in no time. / Mostly Bs: Rising Star! You've mastered the basics of vlogging and picked up a few tricks of the trade; but there's always more that could be done. See you at the top! / Mostly Cs: Keep Practising! Anyone can make a YouTube video these days, but it takes a lot of time and work to rise to the top. Keep at it though; just by taking this quiz you're already on your way.

WHAT

%

ZOË SUGG

ARE YOU?

Zoë Sugg, aka Zoella, is one of the most successful YouTubers in history – but how much are you like her? Could it be that you are kindred spirits? Find out right here with our magical quiz.

AQ:
WHOOPS, you literally said nothing! Your YouTube fave was right there, you got your photo taken together; but you didn't say a word the whole time and it got really awkward. Maybe next time...

- To start over, turn to page 13
- To go back a step, turn to page 34

1 Where do you spend most of your time?

a) **The Sudan**
b) **Go-karting**
c) **Sleeping**
d) **Hanging with friends**
e) **Online**

2 What's your favourite time of year?

a) **Winter**
b) **Spring**
c) **Summer**
d) **Halloween**
e) **Vlogmas**

3 Choose a dog breed.

a) **Lhasa Apso**
b) **Bichon Frise**
c) **Labrador**
d) **Bulldog**
e) **Pug**

4 Pick a type of weather.

a) **Rain**
b) **Overcast**
c) **Mild**
d) **Snow**
e) **Sunshine**

5 Choose a place.

a) **Siberia**
b) **Japan**
c) **London**
d) **Brighton**
e) **The Isle of Wight**

6 What are your favourite kind of days?

a) **Weekdays**
b) **Die Another Days**
c) **Public holidays**
d) **Holidays**
e) **Alfie Deyes**

Mostly As: You are 0% Zoë Sugg. You have absolutely no Sugginess about you. Sorry. / Mostly Bs: You are 25% Zoë Sugg. You might like pugs or perhaps you've visited Brighton. You don't have much in common with Zoe, but you could easily have a chat with her. / Mostly Cs: You are 50% Zoë Sugg. You're halfway there. The question is, is it the top half, or the bottom half? / Mostly Ds: You are 75% Zoë Sugg. You could almost be a sibling or something. Anyone heard of Chloe Sugg? / Mostly Es: You are 100% Zoë Sugg. Are you sure you're not she?

THE HARDEST NIKKIETUTORIALS QUIZ EVER

How much of a NikkieTutorials fan are you? Here are some of the most unknown and downright impossible facts about this amazing beauty YouTuber, and now all YOU need to do is prove that you're her number one fan by getting 100% in this quiz. Sound simple? PROVE IT.

1 What is Nikkie's star sign?
CLUE: She was born in March.

a) **Pisces**
b) **Capricorn**
c) **Aries**

2 She may have an adorable American accent, but where was Nikkie born?

a) **Sweden**
b) **The Netherlands**
c) **Germany**

3 What year did Nikkie start her YouTube channel?

a) **2007**
b) **2008**
c) **2009**

4 What TV show inspired Nikkie to start up her YouTube channel?

a) **The Hills**
b) **90210**
c) **Gossip Girl**

5 What member of her family runs the skincare shop, HetCosmeticaHuis?

a) **Her sister**
b) **Her partner**
c) **Her mother**

6 According to her website, how tall is Nikkie?

a) **5 feet 10 inches**
b) **6 feet**
c) **6 feet 2 inches**

7 Which European capital did Nikkie study makeup in?

a) **Paris**
b) **Amsterdam**
c) **Madrid**

8 And finally, what is by far her most popular video?

a) **The Power Of Makeup**
b) **FULL FACE USING ONLY KIDS MAKEUP Challenge**
c) **FULL FACE USING ONLY LIQUID LIPSTICKS Challenge**

TRUE YOUTUBE FAN! ___ / 8

Turn to page **140** for the answers

CRAZY FAN TICK LIST

You've probably done a lot of things in the name of YouTube that you were hoping to keep secret but now it's time to let everything out of your closet. Tick everything off this list that you've done, no matter how shameful.

1. Attended a meet up or book signing by a YouTuber and cried when you met them

2. Attended a meet-up or book signing by a YouTuber and threw up when you met them (urgh)

3. Baked a cake inspired by a YouTuber, Tweeted it to them and felt satisfied when they RT'd you

4. Been caught sleep-talking about a YouTuber

5. Bought a game because of a YouTuber

6. Bought a ukulele because YouTubers make it look so easy (then never learned to play)

7. Bought an item of clothing because of a YouTuber

8. Bought copies of a YouTuber book as birthday/Christmas gifts for family or friends

9. Bought several beauty products because of a YouTuber

10. Bought YouTuber merch you already owned

11. Called your boyfriend or girlfriend by the name of a YouTuber and not their actual name (double tick if they dumped you as a result)

12. Commented 'Notice me, Senpai!' on a YouTuber's social media post

13. Commented first (shame on you)

14. Commented first and actually been first (seriously, shame on you)

15. Commented first knowing you were not first (you're the worst)

16. Considered changing your last name to Sugg/Deyes/Howell etc. by deed poll

17. Created a fan Twitter account

18. Created an incredibly cringe-worthy email address which references a YouTuber and lived to regret it

19. Created an incredibly cringe-worthy email address which references a YouTuber and applied for a job using said email address

20. Created more than one fan Twitter account

21. Created new YouTube accounts just so you could subscribe to a YouTuber again

22. Developed a deep love of guinea pigs and/or pugs because of Zoë Sugg

23. Friend requested a YouTuber's real Facebook account

24. Gone to Brighton only because of YouTubers

TOTAL: _____

Build A Playlist And We'll Tell You Your Favourite Musical YouTuber

Music and YouTube have always gone hand in hand. From Justin Bieber's very early days to the iconic Todrick Hall, YouTube has literally been music to our ears. So in this new musical quiz you'll create your ultimate 10-track playlist, and your favourite YouTube musical act will be revealed. Simple.

1   Choose one of these songs:

a)   **'Touch' by Little Mix**
b)   **'Summer of '69' by Bryan Adams**
c)   **'Slow Hands' by Niall Horan**
d)   **'Passionfruit' by Drake**
e)   **'Teenagers' by My Chemical Romance**
f)   **'Rock DJ' by Robbie Williams**

2   Pick another:

a)   **'What Now' by Rihanna**
b)   **'Kiss You' by One Direction**
c)   **'Green Light' by Lorde**
d)   **'Work from Home' by Fifth Harmony**
e)   **'Sorry' by Justin Bieber**
f)   **'Hello' by Adele**

3   And pick a third song:

a)   **'I Miss You' by Blink 182**
b)   **'Malibu' by Miley Cyrus**
c)   **'Colors' by Halsey**
d)   **'Did You See' by J HUS**
e)   **'HUMBLE.' by Kendrick Lamar**
f)   **'Friday I'm In Love' by The Cure**

4   Next, pick a Beyoncé song:

a)   **'Daddy Lessons'**
b)   **'Who Run The World (Girls)'**
c)   **'Love On Top'**
d)   **No thanks!**
e)   **'Crazy in Love'**
f)   **'Deja Vu'**

MORE QUESTIONS THIS WAY

➡

5 Pick one of these bangers:

a) 'Hard Times' by Paramore
b) 'Chocolate' by The 1975
c) 'Sign of the Times' by Harry Styles
d) 'Stronger' by Kanye West
e) 'Mr Brightside' by The Killers
f) 'Poker Face' by Lady Gaga

6 Pick a 5SOS song:

a) No thanks!
b) 'She's Kinda Hot'
c) 'Girls Talk Boys'
d) 'Amnesia'
e) 'Jet Black Heart'
f) 'She Looks So Perfect'

7 Now a Panic! song:

a) 'Don't Threaten Me with a Good Time'
b) No thanks!
c) 'This is Gospel'
d) 'Death of a Bachelor'
e) 'I Write Sins Not Tragedies'
f) 'Time to Dance'

After the event is over, your notifications start blowing up – your YouTube fave re-Tweeted you! They jokingly added "looking forward to our second ;)". WOW, you're cool.

- To start over, turn to page 13

8 Pick one of these tracks:

a) **'I Want to Break Free' by Queen**
b) **'24K Magic' by Bruno Mars**
c) **'Don't Wanna Know' by Maroon 5**
d) **'Complicated' by Avril Lavigne**
e) **'Galway Girl' by Ed Sheeran**
f) **'Big for Your Boots' by Stormzy**

9 Pick an Ed Sheeran song:

a) **'Don't'**
b) **No thanks!**
c) **'Shape of You'**
d) **'Lego House'**
e) **'Castle on the Hill'**
f) **'The A Team'**

10 Pick your final song:

a) **'Confident' by Demi Lovato**
b) **'Side To Side' by Ariana Grande**
c) **'Reach' by S Club 7**
d) **'Angels' by Robbie Williams**
e) **'Super Bass' by Nicki Minaj**
f) **'Run Away with Me' by Carly Rae Jepsen**

Mostly As: Emma Blackery / Mostly Bs: Troye Sivan / Mostly Cs: Dodie Clark / Mostly Ds: Andrew Huang / Mostly Es: Jacob Sartorius / Mostly Fs: Pentatonix

Match The (Youtuber) To Their Instagram (Post)

Doing it for the likes! Instagram has given us all the ability to get an extra dose of vlogging action from our favourite creators. But for all the hours you spend scrolling and liking; how well do you really know the themes and aesthetic that belong to your favourite YouTubers?

AQ: You realise there's SO much more to do at this event than just meet and greets. The lines look a little long and boring anyway. Better yet, your YouTube fave is also doing a panel AND a stage performance...

- To wait for the panel, turn to page 74
- To wait at the stage, turn to page 54

Dodie Clark → Laci Green
Zoë Sugg   Nathan Zed
Connor Franta   Phil Lester
Liza Koshy   Gabriella Lindley
Chanel Ambrose →

1

2

3

4

5

6

7

8

9

TRUE YOUTUBE FAN!

___ / 9

Turn to page **140** for the answers

WHO ARE WE TALKING ABOUT?

?

This quiz is less Burn Book and more High School yearbook. You'll have to guess who is being described from a series of famous quotes, cryptic clues and in-jokes that only hardcore fans will get. Your YouTube Fan status depends on how many you get right.

0–4: Oh dear, are you still half asleep? Let's be honest, some of the clues were quite obvious. Why not catch up on the videos in your 'Watch Later' list with a huge cup of coffee and come back and try again?

5–8: Not bad! You're switched on to the in-jokes in the world of YouTube and you were probably kicking yourself when you read some of the answers. Don't worry, it ain't easy getting them all right.

9–12: Are you an actual detective? Because you had those clues FIGURED OUT. You know everything there is to know about the world of YouTube and love geeking out on facts about the world's biggest YouTube stars.

1. This YouTuber's career has blossomed thanks to two very glam books, a lipstick with MAC cosmetics and even her own range of eyelashes.

- - - - - - - - - - - - - - - - -

2. With a famous brother, there's got to be a degree of sibling rivalry for this British creator. He reached one million subscribers in March 2017.

- - - - - - - - - - - - - - - - -

3. She's living the American dream with millions of subscribers, a clothing range and even her own book. Can you 'Make Your Mind Up' on who we're talking about?

- - - - - - - - - - - - - - - - -

4. This British YouTuber gives us the serious 'Feel Good' factor and has more musical talent than a bunch of auto-tuned goats (yes, really).

- - - - - - - - - - - - - - - - -

5. From Vine to YouTube, there's no platform this exceptionally talented man can't take on. Having won the 2017 Shorty Award for 'Best YouTuber Comedian', you can bet he'll win you over with his funny personality and charm.

- - - - - - - - - - - - - - - - -

6. This gaming YouTuber is a sparkling light within the community. And that's the only clue we're going to give you.

- - - - - - - - - - - - - - - - -

7. She's an OG YouTuber who is famous for the cinnamon challenge. As well as being a YouTuber, this person is also a mum to a baby with a name very similar to her own.

- - - - - - - - - - - - - - - - -

8. His real first name is Rolf but he goes by his middle name. You could recognise him just by his 'Sweatshirt'.

- - - - - - - - - - - - - - - - -

9. This couple got married in March 2015 and share very similar names... Which pair do you think we're talking about?

- - - - - - - - - - - - - - - - -

10. As well as working on a YouTube channel and a clothing line, this YouTuber is also mum to Indie-Rose.

- - - - - - - - - - - - - - - - -

11. She's got a LOT of baes and is the most beautiful, talented, perfect person in the entire world (she paid us to write that). Grab your daddy saddle and tell us who we're talking about here.

- - - - - - - - - - - - - - - - -

12. This trans creator came out as a lesbian in September 2016 and has gone on to date an actual billionaire. As well as YouTube, this person released a film called 'This is Everything' in 2017.

- - - - - - - - - - - - - - - - -

TRUE **YOUTUBE** FAN! **___ / 12**

Turn to page **140** for the answers

Can You Match The YouTuber To Their Comments?

Ah, the comment sections. Filled with the wonderful, weird and random musings of fans and critics alike. Here are a bunch of comments that were left on the videos of some of YouTube's top creators. Can you match the comments to the creators and ace the quiz? TBH, it's the only thing that's gonna make you feel like you've achieved something today, so why not take it?

Your waiting paid off – you're right at the front of the crowd when your fave comes on stage! You're pretty sure they can barely see you at all because of the lights. Oh well, at least you got this close, right?

- To start over, turn to page 13
- To go back a step, turn to page 50

1. 'HE LITERALLY NOTICED ME I AM THE BIG D GUY LIKE OMG IM CRAFTING.'

2. 'This comment section is the most positive on youtube. I LOVE IT!!'

3. 'This is so beautiful. I have a feeling I'll be listening to this non-stop for a while.'

4. 'I'm a banana pepper and I'd appreciate it if you didn't question my existence.'

5. 'Sorry if you mention it in this video but what highlighter you wearing in the video? DAT GLOW THO'

6. 'YES! FINALLY THE OG DOABM IS BACK! CAN'T WAIT!'

7. 'Can't wait for vlogmas!'

8. 'I loved this video and it really helped me to understand alot of things especially if im only 13.'

9. 'THAT HAMILTON POSTER TURNT'

Dan Howell

Dodie Clark

Hannah Hart

Humza Productions

Lilly Singh

Mark Ferris

Nathan Zed

Gabriella

Zoella

Turn to page **140** for the answers

___ / 9   TRUE YOUTUBE FAN!

Plan Your Daily Routine And We'll Tell You What Your YouTube Channel Should Be About

When creating your YouTube channel, there's a lot to think about; but most important of all is deciding what to actually make videos about, which is why we suggest playing to your strengths, and basing your videos on what you end up doing every day. So with this handy quiz, you'll discover the perfect video genre for you based solely on what you like to do during the day.

1 What time would you IDEALLY like to wake up?

a) **Late as heck**
b) **Between 8–10 a.m.**
c) **7 a.m. or before**
d) **Sometime before noon**

2 Pick a breakfast.

a) **Last night's pizza**
b) **Cereal**
c) **Avocado and egg on toast**
d) **Coffee**

3 Do you plan on going outside today?

a) **Nope, can't be bothered**
b) **Yep, need the inspiration**
c) **Yep, but only because I need to**
d) **Nope, far too much work to do**

4 What are your lunch plans?

a) **Oh man, I skipped lunch**
b) **Meeting friends**
c) **Cooking something up**
d) **I'll buy a snack**

5 How much time is 'work' time?

a) **All play, baby**
b) **About 1–2 hours**
c) **My life is work**
d) **Up to 6 hours**

6 Pick a dinner.

a) **Takeaway**
b) **At a posh restaurant**
c) **Stir-fry**
d) **Chicken Nuggets**

7 You've got a few hours free in the evening – how do you spend it?

a) **Catching up on social media**
b) **Just daydreaming**
c) **Editing today's footage**
d) **Reading**

8 Lastly, what causes you to go to sleep?

a) **My eyes won't stay open**
b) **Exhaustion**
c) **The need to get up and go out the next day**
d) **A meeting in the morning**

Mostly As: You love to take things easy. You wake late and stay up into the wee hours. You could make a great Gaming or Story Time channel. / Mostly Bs: You're a creative individual so put that talent to good use with a Music or Drama channel. / Mostly Cs: You live your life on the go. There's always something going on so why not start a Lifestyle or Daily Vlogging channel? / Mostly Ds: You're fairly laidback but you're also a hardworking and cultured individual. Why not share your knowledge through a BookTube or Filmmaking channel?

57

CAN YOU MATCH THE REVELMODE ICON TO THE YOUTUBER?

You may be a PewDiePie pro, a Markiplier master or a jacksepticeye genius... but how well do you know the rest of the Revelmode crew? If you don't know what on earth Revelmode is, go check them out on the Revelmode homepage – but after this quiz. Don't cheat!

All you need to do is match the creator to their colourful graphic, which is way harder than you think.

CINNAMONTOASTKEN

CRYAOTIC

CUTIEPIEMARZIA

DODGER

EMMA BLACKERY

JELLY

KICKTHEPJ

PEWDIEPIE

SLOGOMAN

Turn to page **140**
for the answers

___ / **9**

TRUE
YOUTUBE
FAN!

What Will Your

YouTuber

Role Be?

The online community is made up of more than just YouTubers. There are countless roles, both in front of the camera and behind it, that help make your favourite creators' videos magical. It's time to work out which of these roles best suits you. Please bear in mind that this quiz is a legally binding contract, so whatever option you get is the job you will be forced to do henceforth, forever, until the sun itself burns out. HAVE FUN!

AQ:

Now what kind of attitude is that?! You'll never know what adventures could possibly unfold if you actively decide to miss out. Go on, it'll be fun...

- To start over, turn to page 13
- To go back a step, turn to page 32

1 How are you with a camera?

a) **I'm like the Steven Spielberg of YouTube.**
b) **I can shoot straight.**
c) **I can just about manage a still picture.**
d) **My mere presence is enough to destroy nearby technology.**

2 Do you have an in-depth knowledge of what the children refer to as 'memes'?

a) **Why follow memes when you can make your own.**
b) **I can salt bae with the best of them.**
c) **Memes? Hey, that's pretty good.**
d) **My life is a damn meme.**

3 How problematic are you, in any given moment?

a) **I am an angel... let's go with that.**
b) **What can I say? I'm only human.**
c) **Lol, pretty damn problematic.**
d) **I am one of history's greatest monsters.**

4 Would you go so far as to describe yourself as one of history's greatest monsters?

a) **Absolutely.**
b) **Yeah, probably.**
c) **Hmm, not really.**
d) **I literally just did man. Open your ears!**

5 Are you literate?

a) **I don't want to brag but I can read any pamphlet that's put in front of me.**
b) **I love to read and write.**
c) **Why write when an image is worth a thousand words?**
d) **Well, I'm reading this book, ain't I?**

6 You're at a party – what are you most likely doing?

a) **Socialising – or trying to.**
b) **Trying to locate, and then pet, any animals that may be in the house.**
c) **Getting some dope pics so I can flex on the 'gram... I am so alone.**
d) **Lol, me at a party. Good one.**

Mostly As: You're a creative mastermind with the ability to turn light and shadows into audio-visual magic. Get behind the camera as the director of photography. / Mostly Bs: Whether it's helping creators write scripts or ghostwriting entire novels for them (just kidding, that never happens...), writing is the 'write' path for you. / Mostly Cs: You're totally social media savvy. You could be an 'influencer', which is a truly unique career title because it will make you a ton of money just being totally meaningless. / Mostly Ds: Fandom is your true home. You're the loudest to cheer when you see a creator live and the first to attack when trolls come for them on social media.

Are You A Cliché Beauty Blogger?

Every
Beauty
Vlogger

Do you have an obsession with fairy lights? Is your makeup bag your most precious belonging? Are you worried you may be a cliché beauty blogger? Well you don't need to worry anymore. Here's a quiz that will test you on just that.

1

Do you have A LOT of fairy lights in your bedroom?

a) **I really do!**
b) **Nope, no fairy lights.**

2

How big is your makeup bag?

a) **It's the biggest bag I own.**
b) **It's a big bag, but not TOO big!**

3

Is it possible for you to live without lipstick in your life?

a) **I mean, no.**
b) **If it had to be done, I could do it.**

4

Are Zoella's beauty hauls your most watched videos on YouTube?

a) **Yes, and I have no shame in it.**
b) **I watch a lot of different things because I'm cool like that.**

5

If you had a £10 makeup voucher what product would you spend it on?

a) **A new beauty blender to achieve an amazing contour.**
b) **A nice, pretty smelling moisturiser.**

6

Is contouring life?

a) **Obviously.**
b) **It's not EVERYTHING.**

7

Do you have a random plant in the corner of your room?

a) **It looks good in the background of selfies.**
b) **No, that seems pointless.**

8

Do you get all your interior design ideas off Pinterest?

a) **Pinterest is everything.**
b) **I create my own ideas.**

9

Are there a lot of Polaroid pictures on your bedroom walls tied together with pretty string?

a) **Yeah, I saw it on Pinterest once.**
b) **There are some, but I have other things like posters up too.**

 Mostly As: You're a cliché beauty blogger! / Mostly Bs: You've got your own unique style!

IS THIS THE NAME OF A VIDEO GAME OR A YOUTUBE CHANNEL?

Let's be completely real before we start this quiz; names from both the video game and YouTube world are equally stupid. What does PewDiePie even mean? Or CinnamonToastKen? Or Sonic the Hedgehog for that matter? Either way, stupid names for both of these creative outlets exist, but this quiz is designed to see if you can spot the difference between the two.

Here are 10 weird and wonderful names from the world of video games and YouTubers, and all you need to do is figure out whether the name belongs to a game or a YouTube channel.

1. 'Tongue of the Fatman'

Video Game ☐   YouTube Channel ☐

2. 'Manly Badass Hero'

Video Game ☐   YouTube Channel ☐

3. 'TetraNinja'

Video Game ☐   YouTube Channel ☐

4. 'Princess Tomato in Salad Kingdom'

Video Game ☐   YouTube Channel ☐

5. 'Jelly'

Video Game ☐   YouTube Channel ☐

6. 'Ninja Hamster'

Video Game ☐   YouTube Channel ☐

7. 'Life of Tom'

Video Game ☐   YouTube Channel ☐

8. ''Splosion Man'

Video Game ☐   YouTube Channel ☐

9. 'Ninjabread Man'

Video Game ☐   YouTube Channel ☐

10. 'MrSuicideSheep'

Video Game ☐   YouTube Channel ☐

TRUE YOUTUBE FAN! ___ / 10

Turn to page **140** for the answers

How Many Gaming YouTubers Can You Find In This Word Search?

Here's a new challenge, and it's one that doesn't require a deep knowledge of YouTubers and their many various interests or body parts. Your challenge is to spot a huge bunch of gaming YouTubers in the word search, but here's the tricky part... you don't know how many there are to find. Write down the YouTubers as you find them.

AQ:

You suggest doing a crazy pose with your YouTuber fave – and in response, they suddenly get down on one knee. And you just BURST out crying. You might not look cool, but you're definitely memorable...

- To start over, turn to page 13
- To go back a step, turn to page 16

```
G K X P N F E J P B L C Z Y L S H X U G C N U J K
C L G U C N S C A P T A I N S P A R K L E Z X A S
J W T L U X M B Q F M F M T L Z N P A D N O Z C C
J T H H Z M O J E H N E U I H A S C U P Q U A K E
V W D V E F S B A U A R U E K A Y D K W P X U S N
B Z B C A C H P F L G M U S M P B H S X P Y K E S
Y K L Z M F G R F P M A D T H A I Y Y E S L D P U
Q Y Q L A X A O I Q L N F A P D S R E B R G B T K
F E Z F R G M S M M D F H M B G V V A Z J L T I F
P G K D K C E Y P Q S L M P P I A I S N N A A C R
L V Y S I V S N L D H O S Y O Z N L S C P I U E V
A O W S P I E D I T A O B L P N O D F T L O E Y J
W J N P L H D I V X D X W O U E S V A A A J R E R
M T N A I K J C J F O X S N L R S M K D G Z J V I
N Y M K E U A A C G W A S G A V G G H S B H C V S
Z S B F R E G T D X L W S H R H A Y O S L W M V X
Y B V A W Q M E H T A E N E M X M H V X W N A N O
G P E W D I E P I E D R I A M Y I S E Y Z H I X Z
H A S M N D H K T L Y I P D O D N E V I E M A G R
W U W C V B P F I V K I E G S T G J N S G B D A I
G W O K V B B Y X J S Q R S L H K O D P J X P D L
U H B A E E O D T K M F W O Q U B D R R E N R E U
S S E A N A N N E R S H O R A F U E D W H O V H B
H E Q A Y O G S C A S T L M A D H G A U V F E D P
N S H P Q S N D N S Q I F P D T N B O R B E J Z U
```

------------------   ------------------   ------------------

------------------   ------------------   ------------------

------------------   ------------------   ------------------

------------------   ------------------   ------------------

------------------   ------------------   ------------------

Turn to page **140** for the answers

MATCH THE YOUTUBER TO THEIR BOOK TITLE

The year 2016 was truly the year ~~of the deaths of beloved celebrities~~ YouTuber books – but just how well have you been keeping track of all these literary classics? It's time to find out. Can you match the creator to the title of their creation? Things are getting literally literary!

1. Hello Life

BETHANY MOTA

2. Girl Online

CHARLIE MCDONNELL

3. Selp-Helf

4. Binge

CONNOR FRANTA

5. Fun Science:
A Guide To Life,
The Universe And
Why Science Is So
Awesome

DAN AND PHIL

MARCUS BUTLER

6. A Work in Progress

MIRANDA SINGS

7. Generation Next

OLI WHITE

8. The Amazing Book
is Not on Fire

TYLER OAKLEY

9. Make Your Mind Up

ZÖE SUGG

TRUE YOUTUBE FAN!

___ / 9

Turn to page **141** for the answers

WHO IS OLDER?

CELEBRITIES VS YOUTUBERS

Do YouTubers ever age? When you think about it, so many of our faves have been on the platform for around 10 years and yet they've all got perfect skin and literally zero pores. And the same goes for celebrities – how can they be so young, yet so successful?! But can you tell who is older: our beloved YouTubers or favourite celebrities?

Who is older?
Dan Howell or Selena Gomez

Who is older?
Liza Koshy or Charlie Puth

It's the battle of the blondes...
Niomi Smart or Taylor Swift

Who is older?
Miles McKenna or Willow Smith

What about...
Phil Lester or Cristiano Ronaldo?

How about these lovely ladies?
Lilly Singh or Hilary Duff

Any idea?
Hannah Witton or Zayn Malik

Who is older?
Grace Victory or Perrie Edwards

Which one was born first?
Caspar Lee or Niall Horan

Finally, who is older?
Lele Pons or Kylie Jenner

TRUE
YOUTUBE
FAN!

___ / 10

Turn to page **141**
for the answers

Match These YouTubers To Their Hometowns

There's nothing like a bit of hometown pride. Remember when jacksepticeye's local paper realised just how famous he was and did the sweetest feature on him? Or how everyone in Brighton hates the fact the city is known as 'YouTuber World' now?

Whether you're from Buckinghamshire and reppin' Oli White or picked the university you go to based on the fact Phil Lester studied there, it's time to take a geography lesson and match the YouTuber to their hometown.

Simply draw a line between the YouTubers and their place on the map.

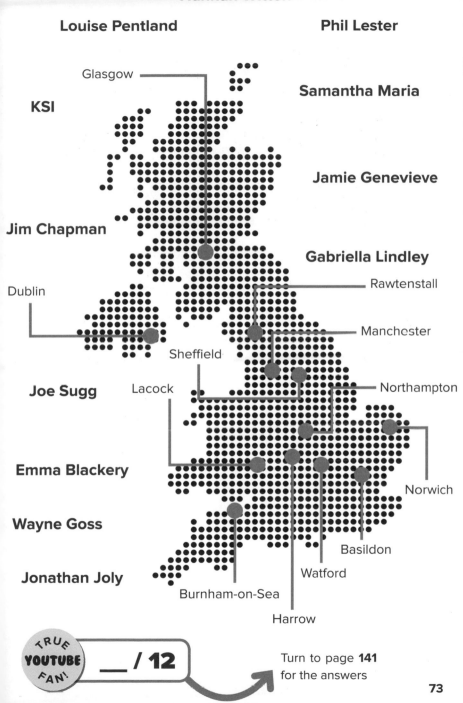

Hannah Witton

Louise Pentland

Phil Lester

Samantha Maria

KSI

Jamie Genevieve

Glasgow

Jim Chapman

Gabriella Lindley

Rawtenstall

Dublin

Manchester

Sheffield

Joe Sugg

Lacock

Northampton

Emma Blackery

Wayne Goss

Norwich

Jonathan Joly

Basildon

Watford

Burnham-on-Sea

Harrow

__ / 12

TRUE YOUTUBE FAN!

Turn to page **141** for the answers

CAN YOU GUESS THE YOUTUBER WE'VE PIXELATED?

Nine of your favourite YouTube creators have been pixelated to try and confuse you – so if you can decipher the pixels, then you're gonna nail this quiz. Have a look at these pixelated images and see if you can work out which YouTuber it is. Simply match the name to the pixel perfect picture.

AQ:

There are a LOT of people waiting for this panel to start – your YouTube fave is the most popular person at this event. But as the speakers approach the table from backstage, you're the first person to see them! What do you do?

- To scream in excitement, turn to page 84
- To wave and hope they notice, turn to page 94

Dodie Clark

Elijah Daniel

iHasCupquake

Joey Graceffa

Zoë Sugg

Caspar Lee

Scola Dondo

Shane Dawson

Tana Mongeau

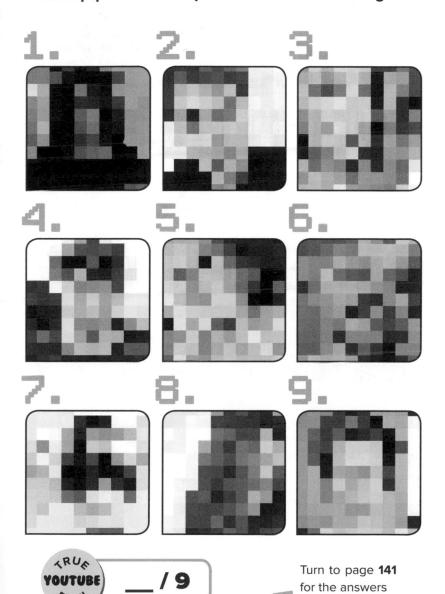

TRUE YOUTUBE FAN!

___ / 9

Turn to page **141** for the answers

ARE YOU HAVING AN EXISTENTIAL CRISIS RIGHT NOW?

If you don't know what an existential crisis is, you can get clued up by watching Dan Howell's video explaining it all. Once you know what you're dealing with, it's time to take our quiz. Is the weight of the world on your shoulders?

What is the meaning of life?

a) **Nothing. Life is pointless.**
b) **To keep on truckin'.**
c) **Delicious bread.**

What does it all mean?

a) **WHO KNOWS?!**
b) **I don't know, but I can't wait to find out.**
c) **IDK, but I'm going to just keep swimming.**

Finish these lyrics: 'When I was a young boy / My father took me into the city...'

a) **'...to see a marching band.'**
b) **I don't know this song.**
c) **I don't know what music is.**

How much time do you spend lying on the floor?

a) **My whole life.**
b) **None! :)**
c) **I spend most of my time in water.**

WHYYYY??

a) **WHHHYYYY!**
b) **Chin up, pal!**
c) **I'm just wingin' it.**

The world is...

a) **Dark and unforgiving.**
b) **Full of opportunity.**
c) **My airport.**

Finish these lyrics: 'Somebody once told me the world is gonna roll me...'

a) **I don't know that song.**
b) **'...I ain't the sharpest tool in the shed.'**
c) ***honk***

Mostly As: CHAOS! DARKNESS! AHHHHHHHHHH! It appears as if you are having a crisis – of the "existential" variety. Guess you have no choice but to lay down on the floor and let the wave of internal terror wash over you like some kind of wave. / Mostly Bs: You are at peace with the state of the universe. Your existence is something you not only comprehend but enjoy and appreciate. Hooray for existing! / Mostly Cs: Huh. I don't think any of us saw this coming but the results don't lie – you're a goose. Better go to a pond and do some goose stuff I guess.

JennaMarbles
True 👍
Or
👎 False

She's an OG of YouTube and was the first big YouTube celebrity to hit the mainstream. With her charm and wit and entourage of smiling dogs, JennaMarbles is a YouTube icon. So, can you guess whether these facts about Jenna are true or false?

Total up your score out of 10 to find out how much of a Jenna stan you are, then don't forget to add it to your True YouTube Fan scoresheet.

1 JennaMarbles once successfully attached her dog to many helium balloons in a bid to make it fly.

True ☐   False ☐

2 Jenna has a degree in fashion design and designed the wedding dress of Catherine Middleton, the Duchess of Cambridge.

True ☐   False ☐

3 So well-known and adored is she in Japan, Jenna has a ramen restaurant themed around her.

True ☐   False ☐

4 Before she was famous, Jenna worked as a go-go dancer, a bartender and a tanning salon assistant.

True ☐   False ☐

5 JennaMarbles' very first collab video was with Jacob Sartorious. They baked fidget spinner cookies together.

True ☐   False ☐

6 In a video, Jenna once covered her entire face in sparkly rhinestones for absolutely no viable reason.

True ☐   False ☐

7 JennaMarbles has her own range of dog toys called 'Kermie Worm And Mr Marbles'

True ☐   False ☐

8 According to Jenna, her dream dinner party guests would include the person who invented Pokémon, Zoë Sugg, the entire We The Unicorns team and her dogs.

True ☐   False ☐

9 Jenna married her partner Julian in a romantic ceremony in Hawaii where she wore a traditional grass skirt.

True ☐   False ☐

10 Jenna is related to fellow YouTuber DanTDM – he's her third cousin once removed.

True ☐   False ☐

TRUE YOUTUBE FAN!   ___ / 10

Turn to page **141** for the answers

MATCH THE YOUTUBER TO THEIR SURNAME

Now, you might be reading the title of this quiz and wondering what fools would dare test your knowledge in such ways. Of course you know your Suggs from your Howells, your Singhs from your Lees and your Oakleys from your Mongeaus but you'd actually be surprised at how many YouTubers don't shout their last name from the rooftops.

Nic, Pixiwoo   Coburn

 Nathan Zed   Connell

 TomSka   Fischbach

 Inthefrow   Fuentes

 I Covet Thee   Gardner

 KathleenLights   Haste

 jacksepticeye   Magrath

 Markiplier   McLoughlin

 Lucy and Lydia   Porteous

 Amelia Liana   Ridgewell

 Just Jodes   Sopher

 The Anna Edit   Zelalem

TRUE YOUTUBE FAN!   __ / 12

Turn to page **141** for the answers

WHAT PERCENTAGE PURE TRASH ARE YOU ?

It's time to get real kids, being a fangirl is just a part of life and the sooner you come to understand that the better. Simply answer the six very basic but highly scientific questions to find out what percentage trash you are. Don't forget to test your family and friends so you can all find out where you rank on the garbage scale!

Warning: Please don't eat literal trash. You're worth more than that to us.

1 How many times a day do you physically consume garbage?

a) Never, TBH.
b) Most meals.
c) ... there's another food group?

2 Honestly, have you ever screamed the words "OTP" out loud?

a) I tried it once and HATED IT.
b) A couple of times, but only ironically.
c) There are other words in the dictionary?

3 How would you react if your fave appeared in front of you, right this second?

a) I'd be chill on the outside, but...
b) I'd be emotional both inside and out.
c) Is there any other option but to FREAK OUT?!

4 Would you ever sacrifice your soul for your fave?

a) Nah, I'm number one.
b) Maybe, like half my soul. I'll think about it.
c) You mean some people wouldn't?!

5 Would you ever use the label "trash" to describe yourself with pride?

a) Only on anonymous message boards.
b) Only with friends...
c) I'LL WEAR IT LIKE A BADGE OF HONOUR.

6 Lastly, how many ships do you belong to right now?

a) None. I'm not a shipper, really.
b) Oh a couple, easily.
c) AS MANY AS EMOTIONALLY POSSIBLE.

Work out your % of trash:
For every A answer add 3,
For every B answer add 9,
For every C answer add 17.

I am _____ %
Pure Trash!

*Yes, you can be OFF THE SCALE, you garbage human!

HOW MANY OF THESE 75 HUGE CHANNELS ARE YOU ACTUALLY SUBSCRIBED TO?

You may be subscribed to a small handful of creators you watch religiously. Or perhaps, you'll click that subscribe button like no one is watching and have a mountain of 'watch later' videos waiting for you at all times. Let's find out exactly how much of a YouTube superfan you really are. Simply tick off how many of these 75 channels you're subbed to and add up your total at the end to reveal your result. Sorry subscription addicts, this doesn't count towards your scoresheet.

AQ:

Your excitement in the crowd is apparently way too infectious; everyone around you suddenly starts screaming and rushes towards the YouTuber! As security tries to block you all off, you see your idol get rushed away backstage. It'll be a while before they do another public event...

- To start over, turn to page 13
- To go back a step, turn to page 74/page 16

☐	1. Alfie Deyes	☐	25. Hannah Hart	☐	51. Oli White
☐	2. AmazingPhil	☐	26. Ingrid Nilsen	☐	52. Paint
☐	3. Aspyn Ovard	☐	27. Jack Maynard	☐	53. PTXOfficial
☐	4. Bethany Mota	☐	28. jacksepticeye	☐	54. PewDiePie
☐	5. Carrie Hope Fletcher (ItsWay-PastMyBedtime)	☐	29. Jake Paul	☐	55. pixiwoo
		☐	30. jeffreestar	☐	56. Ricky Dillon
☐	6. Casey Neistat	☐	31. JennaMarbles	☐	57. Roman Atwood
☐	7. Caspar Lee	☐	32. Jim Chapman	☐	58. Rosanna Pansino
☐	8. Charlie McDonnell (Charlieissocoollike)	☐	33. Joe Sugg	☐	59. Rose and Rosie
		☐	34. Joey Graceffa	☐	60. Ryan Higa
☐	9. Connor Franta	☐	35. Kandee Johnson	☐	61. Ryan ToysReview
☐	10. DanAndPhilGames	☐	36. KickThePj	☐	62. SACCONEJOLYs
☐	11. DanTDM	☐	37. KSI	☐	63. Samantha Maria
☐	12. Daniel Howell	☐	38. Kwebbelkop	☐	64. Shane
☐	13. Dodie Clark	☐	39. LaurDIY	☐	65. Smosh
☐	14. Emma Blackery	☐	40. Lilly Singh	☐	66. SprinkleofChatter
☐	15. Epic Rap Battles	☐	41. Liza Koshy	☐	67. stampylonghead
☐	16. Estée Lalonde	☐	42. Louise Pentland	☐	68. Tanya Burr
☐	17. Fine Brothers	☐	43. LucyAndLydia	☐	69. Thomas Sanders
☐	18. Fleur DeForce	☐	44. Mamrie Hart	☐	70. TomSka
☐	19. Gabriella Lindley	☐	45. Mark Ferris	☐	71. Toys AndMe
☐	20. GameGrumps	☐	46. Markiplier	☐	72. Troye Sivan
☐	21. Gigi Gorgeous	☐	47. Michelle Phan	☐	73. Tyler Oakley
☐	22. GloZell	☐	48. Miranda Sings	☐	74. VanossGaming
☐	23. Grace Helbig	☐	49. More Zoella	☐	75. Zoella
☐	24. Guava Juice	☐	50. Niomi Smart		

___/75

Score: 1–25: You've got niche taste. You know exactly what you like and you stick to it. You tend to only subscribe to YouTubers from one genre, but why not check out some of the other names on this list? You might just find your new favourite. / 26-50: You've got a great balance. You're subscribed to a few of the big names on YouTube but you're also open to trying new creators and smaller channels which is a brilliant way to enjoy YouTube. / 51-75: YouTube is your life. You're utterly addicted to YouTube and love nothing more than finding a new channel and binge-watching all the videos on it. Not only are you totally obsessed with all of the big names, you've also got the up-and-coming stars on your radar. You're a YouTube addict.

How Well Do You Know The Lyrics To 'Friday' By Rebecca Black?

When Rebecca Black's iconic song 'Friday' hit the Internet in 2011, life was changed forever. No longer would the fifth day of the week or cereal be the same again. And whilst you may think you've got the bop eternally stuck in your head, do you really remember it correctly?

Can you fill in the missing lyrics below? Take this quiz no matter what day of the week.

1 'Seven a.m., waking up in the morning
Gotta be ___, gotta go downstairs'

a) **Awake**
b) **Dressed**
c) **Fresh**
d) **Alive**

2 'Gotta get down to the ___'

a) **Bus stop**
b) **School yard**
c) **Parking lot**
d) **Drug store**

3 'Which ___ can I take?'

a) **Spot**
b) **Cake**
c) **Space**
d) **Seat**

4 '7:45, we're drivin' on the ___'

a) **Wrong side**
b) **Highway**
c) **Main road**
d) **Side street**

5 'Fun, fun, ___, fun'

a) **Fun**
b) **Pun**
c) **Bun**
d) **Nun**

6 '___ in the front seat'

a) **Kissin'**
b) **Kickin'**
c) **Chillin'**
d) **Singin'**

7 'We gonna have a ___ today'

a) **Party**
b) **Baby**
c) **Prom**
d) **Ball**

8 'I don't want this ___ to end'

a) **Weekend**
b) **Friday**
c) **Party**
d) **Journey**

9 Gotta get down on ___'

a) **Thursday**
b) **Friday**
c) **Limbo**
d) **The weekend**

TRUE YOUTUBE FAN!

___ / 9

Turn to page **141** for the answers

WHICH YOUTUBE GAMER ARE YOU?

So, you've memorised every PewDiePie and Markiplier fact ever? Now, for your next challenge...

What really matters is seeing how your personality traits align with your YouTube gaming faves, in order to determine which one you are more like. So let's not waste any more time on this introduction and get to the quizzing.

AQ: The YouTuber loves your story! They laugh and say "I guess this is our first date as well!" WHAT. EVEN. Are they flirting? Is this really happening? What's your next move before you go?

- To give them your phone number, turn to page 98
- To Tweet about your "first date" later, turn to page 48

If you could only play one of these games forever, which would it be?

a) **Amnesia: The Dark Descent**
b) **Five Nights at Freddy's**
c) **Happy Wheels**
d) **Far Cry 4**
e) **Minecraft**
f) **Queen Elsa at the Dentist**
g) **Prop Hunt**
h) **Undertale**

What is your favourite genre of video games?

a) **Funny, glitchy simulators**
b) **Games full of jump-scares**
c) **Mature, adult games**
d) **Big, exploratory games**
e) **Building games**
f) **Retro games**
g) **18+ gore**
h) **Survival horror**

The newest Call of Duty game comes out; what do you do?

a) **Mock it endlessly in my videos**
b) **Call of Duty is so commercial**
c) **Highlight all of its flaws to anyone who will listen**
d) **Play and Tweet, play and Tweet! #hype**
e) **Play it – but with loads of mods**
f) **Ignore it entirely and play some weird indie game**
g) **Turn it on and see if it meets your high standards of play**
h) **Play it immediately so I'm on the hype train**

What would your most popular videos be?

a) **Straight talking vlogs**
b) **Montages**
c) **Playing unknown games**
d) **Multiplayer marathon**
e) **Niche game tutorials**
f) **My best bits**
g) **Collab videos with all my famous friends**
h) **Personal vlogs**

MORE QUESTIONS THIS WAY

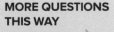

Once a week, you don't post a Let's Play video – what would your upload be instead?

a) Me doing stupid stuff
b) Commenting on world events
c) Directly responding to the week's events
d) A personal video to talk to my fans
e) Is there another kind of video?
f) My comedy genius
g) I don't post many personal videos – it's all about the games
h) An important video about a topic I'm passionate about

What is your strongest emotion?

a) The ability to not give a monkeys
b) Fear
c) Confusion
d) Hyperactivity
e) Indifference
f) Sugar highs
g) Anxiety
h) That feeling you get when you can't make a decision

Do you have much free time?

a) I make sure to eat and sleep, but that's it
b) I don't need free time
c) I'm an insomniac
d) Meal times are sacred
e) YouTube doesn't monopolise my time, I love it
f) I like to have a break from it all now and then
g) I make sure to leave room for free time
h) YouTube is super easy and takes me no time at all

Mostly As... PewDiePie

Mostly Bs... Markiplier

Mostly Cs... jacksepticeye

Mostly Ds... theRadBrad

Mostly Es... LDShadowLady

Mostly Fs... iHasCupquake

Mostly Gs... TheRPGMinx

Mostly Hs... PressHeartToContinue

WHAT % PHIL LESTER ARE YOU?

We could all do with being a bit more like Phil, but just how amazing are ya?

1 How do you feel about beans?

a)   **Meh!**
b)   **I loathe beans**
c)   **Gimme a huge bean!**
d)   **I prefer them on the smaller side**
e)   **I like 'em smol!**

2 Pick an animal:

a)   **Meh!**
b)   **Scorpion**
c)   **Goose**
d)   **Lion**
e)   **Dan Howell**

3 How are we feeling about fringes today?

a)   **Meh!**
b)   **No thank you, Sir**
c)   **They're great, mine goes to the left**
d)   **Love me a fringe**
e)   **I want them straightened and I want them swept to the right and I want that NOW!**

4 Pick your favourite household item:

a)   **Meh!**
b)   **A Sharpie**
c)   **An eclipse T-shirt**
d)   **A craft kit**
e)   **A ladder**

5 Choose something to watch:

a)   **Meh!**
b)   **Hair straightening tutorials**
c)   **The Lion King**
d)   **The Sims Let's Play videos**
e)   **The Weakest Link**

6 Choose a favourite state of being:

a)   **Meh!**
b)   **Cryin'**
c)   **Singing about ladders**
d)   **Crafting**
e)   **Not on fire**

7 What do you not leave home without?

a)   **Meh!**
b)   **A smile**
c)   **Lion the lion**
d)   **Sharpie whiskers**
e)   **My best friend Dan Howell**

Mostly As: You are 0% Phil Lester. There's nothing Amazing or Philly about you. We might as well call you BoringMike. Boo. / Mostly Bs: You are 25% Phil Lester. Which is like an arm, or something. / Mostly Cs: You are 50% Phil Lester. You get to choose top, bottom, left or right. / Mostly Ds: You are 75% Phil Lester. Draw some whiskers on and you may achieve 100%. / Mostly Es: You are 100% Phil Lester. In fact, are you the man himself? Rawr!

93

Odd One

Out

Time for an incredibly serious academic exercise which will demand your full attention. Opposite there are 10 groups of YouTubers and it's your job to tell which one is the odd one out in each group. So just try your best, okay kiddo?

AQ: You wave to your YouTube fave, and as luck would have it, you catch their eye! They smile and wave back just before the crowd loses their mind at the sight of them. And as the panel carries on, you're almost sure they keep looking in your direction. Congrats, you cool cat.

• To start over, turn to page 13

1

Which of these YouTubers is not, primarily, a gamer?

a) jacksepticeye
b) Markiplier
c) charlieissocoollike

2

Which of the these YouTubers is known for their crafting skills?

a) Nathan Zed
b) Phil Lester
c) Humza Productions

3

Which of these YouTubers has not yet released a single?

a) Marcus Butler
b) Emma Blackery
c) Joe Sugg

4

Which of these YouTubers is not Canadian?

a) Lilly Singh
b) Matthew Santoro
c) Shane Dawson

5

Which of these YouTubers has a Master's degree?

a) Jon Cozart
b) JennaMarbles
c) Louise Pentland

6

Which of these YouTubers has more than three million subscribers?

a) Kingsley
b) Dodie Clark
c) communitychannel

7

Which of these YouTubers is, arguably, Tyler Oakley?

a) Ryan Higa
b) Hannah Hart
c) Tyler Oakley

8

Which of these YouTubers has a series called 'As seen on TV'?

a) Casey Neistat
b) h3h3Productions
c) grav3yardgirl

9

Which of these YouTubers is not Australian?

a) Jamie's World
b) Natalie Tran
c) The RackaRacka

10

Which of these fandoms are the most terrifying?

a) The Phandom, obviously
b) Jake Paulers
c) Mirfandas

TRUE YOUTUBE FAN!

___ / 10

Turn to page 141 for the answers

MATCH THE YOUTUBER TO THEIR SONG LYRIC

YouTubers have many talents – including music! A ton of YouTube musicians over the years have created some pretty damn awesome unique sonic creations – the question is, how well do you know them? Find out right here, then log your score on the True YouTube Fan scoresheet on page 137.

TRUE YOUTUBE FAN!

___ / 9

Turn to page **141** for the answers

'Hey, where my baes at? Where my baes at?'

 'Chocolate Rain, Some stay dry and others feel the pain.'

 'Don't wait for the world to be ready, Who says you can't explore?'

 'Welcome, Welcome to the YouTube Culture, The YouTube Cult.'

 'She smells like lemongrass and peach, She tastes like apple juice and peach.'

 'I've got so many chains that I wear around my neck, And I'm so above the game it's like you're watching Star Trek.'

 'So kiss me in the doorway, Always on your way out.'

 'If a girl won't come round, (She must be a lesbian).'

 'We'll take to feet and we'll, Race up the street.'

Dodie Clark   **Julia Nunes**   **Marcus Butler**

Jon Cozart   **Miranda Sings**   **Tay Zonday**

Joey Graceffa   **The Midnight Beast**   **Tessa Violet**

WHO IS YOUR YOUTUBE 👀 BEAUTY 👀 EYE-CON

Check out that pun! With this quiz you'll be well on your way to figuring out which YouTuber is your makeup icon. If you've spent a lifetime watching tutorials and hauls then you'll be well versed in perfecting the eyeliner flick or creating the perfect contoured crease. But which YouTuber is your beauty icon?

AQ:

You quickly write down your number and offer it to them – and they... seem really surprised?!

"Oh! N-no thanks," they say with a smile, as the meet and greet staff usher you away for the next person's turn.

H U M I L I A T I N G.

- To start over, turn to page 13
- To go back a step, turn to page 88

1 Pick a YouTuber to hang out with for the day...

a) **PewDiePie**

b) **Jim Chapman**

c) **Bertie Gilbert**

d) **Amelia Liana**

e) **Tanya Burr**

f) **Grace Helbig**

2 You're on a night out, what shoes are you wearing?

a)

b)

c)

d)

e)

f)

3 What's your ideal way to spend a Saturday night?

a) **At a club dancing all night**

b) **Spending time with family**

c) **At a gig**

d) **At a fancy restaurant**

e) **Disney movies and pizza**

f) **Chilling on your own**

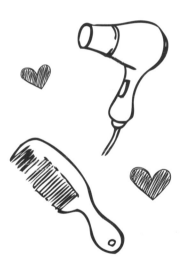

MORE QUESTIONS THIS WAY

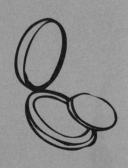

4 Who would you love to see live the most?

a) **Little Mix**

d) **Busted**

b) **Shawn Mendes**

e) **Zayn Malik**

c) **The 1975**

f) **Ariana Grande**

5 Finally, which of these women is your style icon?

a) **Sia**

d) **Kate Middleton**

b) **Marilyn Monroe**

e) **Perrie Edwards**

c) **Twiggy**

f) **Beyonce**

Mostly As... Marzia

Mostly Ds... Fleur DeForce

Mostly Bs... Pixiwoo

Mostly Es... Zoë Sugg

Mostly Cs... Savannah Brown

Mostly Fs... Grace Victory

YouTube Adventure Quiz: Can You Make It As A YouTuber On Tour?

Hopefully by now you've gotten the gist of our YouTube Adventure Quiz; so it's time for you to embark on another exciting saga.

Here's how it works:

- Read the scenario below, and the options for what to do next.
- Pick an option and turn to the corresponding page.
- Repeat as necessary until you reach the end.
- Congrats! You've built a whole story.

In this epic saga, you play the role of a famous YouTuber, off on your very first tour around the UK. Is it for a book? For music? Just for meet-ups? That's up to you. But the story lies in the first decision you make...

1: START

The limited amount of tour time means you have to choose between two major cities: one you used to live in when you started YouTube, and a much bigger city where you might sell more merch/books/etc. Which do you choose?

- To pick your old home city, turn to page 104
- To go to the bigger city, turn to page 108

AQ:

Look out for the adventure quiz boxes throughout the book. There are two adventures, one starting here and the other on page 12. Good luck, and don't mess it up!

CAN YOU MATCH THE YOUTUBER TO THEIR NICKNAME?

Everyone has cute names for their friends and family but what about YouTubers? Do you know the nicknames they get called behind closed doors? It's time to put yourself to the test in the ultimate YouTube nickname quiz.

AQ:

The people of your old hometown are really excited to see you! The show has one of the best vibes of the tour – but the smaller venue means there were fewer sales. Your management suggest adding an extra date to the tour, but you're starting to feel pretty tired from being on the road. What do you do?

- To add an extra date, turn to page 112
- To accept the loss in sales, turn to page 114

1	**Stone Girl**	Carrie Hope Fletc...
2	**Broseph**	Connor Franta
3	**Connie Frannie**	Dan Howell
4	**Bear**	Gabriella Lindley
5	**Kloanda**	GloZell Green
6	**Tilly**	Joe Sugg
7	**Swish**	Louise Pentland
8	**Soups**	PJ Liguori
9	**Peej**	Tyler Oakley

TRUE YOUTUBE FAN!

___ / 9

Turn to page **141** for the answers

COULD YOU REALLY MAKE IT AS A DAILY VLOGGER?

Vlogging: it's hard work. Some days you have no fresh ideas, some days you feel like you don't look camera-ready, and some days you just can't be bothered. So how do people manage to do it daily? This quiz will put your daily vlogging aptitude to the test. Have you got the chops to document every moment of your life for your adoring audience? Time to find out.

AQ: The Tweet didn't do much to quell the people outside; but you've had such a dramatic night that your manager tells you there has been an even bigger demand for you to tour other parts of the world! Next stop, Europe...

- To start over, turn to page 103

1

What are your daily vlogs about?

a) **Sharing my day-to-day life, no matter how boring.**
b) **Vlogging about any old subject, posted daily!**
c) **Umm?? I'll wing it!**
d) **Documenting how much better my life is than yours.**

2

What's the MOST important thing you have to do today?

a) **Get dressed.**
b) **Go to work/school.**
c) **Go shopping.**
d) **Go outside.**

3

Something REALLY important just happened and you missed filming it! What do you do?

a) **Film yourself telling the story of what happened.**
b) **Get everyone and everything involved to recreate it in detail.**
c) **Cry for an hour and delete your channel.**
d) **Pretend it never happened for the rest of your life.**

4

What's the biggest thing to gain from running a daily vlog?

a) **Views.**
b) **Friends.**
c) **Memories.**
d) **Subscribers.**

5

You've been invited to a huge birthday party tonight! What's thing you're most worried about

a) **Will I have time to edit and upload?**
b) **Will I know anybody else going?**
c) **What will I wear?**
d) **Should I take my camera?**

6

What do you like to film with?

a)   c)

b)   d)

7

You forgot to charge your camera last night! What do you do now?

a) **Charge it and film just half of the day.**
b) **Take a day off!**
c) **Go back to bed.**
d) **Panic-buy a new camera.**

8

Who's in your daily vlogging squad?

a) **All my daily vlogging pals.**
b) **My bf/gf/other <3.**
c) **Just me, baby.**
d) **Whoever I'm with!**

Mostly As: You've got the time, the confidence and the motivation for vlogging your entire life, and you always make sure a video goes out every day. / Mostly Bs: You REALLY wanna share your life with the world, but there's all those other obligations holding you back! Maybe for now you you should focus on a weekly schedule of awesome videos? / Mostly Cs: Who needs to vlog DAILY? You make stuff because you enjoy it, not because you feel like you have to! Your audience knows you have a life outside YouTube, they can wait... / Mostly Ds: Okay, so you have a daily vlogging channel; only the actual amount that you stick to "daily" has become something of a running joke between you and your audience.

HOW MUCH DO YOU REALLY KNOW ABOUT DODIE CLARK?

Dodie Clark is one of the most famous musicians on the Internet; from her beautifully written lyrics to her emotional and moving performances, there seems to be nothing this girl can't do. This quiz is all about testing your knowledge of Dodie and finding out just how much of a superfan you really are.

AQ: The event at the larger city was a big success! But you've noticed online that a lot of people from your hometown feel snubbed; they believe you think you've gotten "too big" for them, and are now just in it for the money. How do you respond to clear things up?

- To reply to someone directly, turn to page 116
- To post a public statement, turn to page 124

1 Dodie's real first name is...

a) Dorothy
b) Daniella
c) Denise
d) Deborah

2 What year did Dodie win a Shorty Award for 'YouTube Musician'?

a) 2014
b) 2015
c) 2016
d) 2017

3 What is the name of Dodie's manager?

a) Herbert
b) Peter
c) Joshua
d) Christopher

4 Which of these instruments can Dodie NOT play?

a) Saxophone
b) Ukulele
c) Piano
d) Clarinet

5 Who did Dodie perform 'An Awkward Duet' with?

a) Bry
b) Dan Howell
c) Emma Blackery
d) Jon Cozart

6 What is the name of Dodie's 2016 EP?

a) YouTube Made Me Do It
b) Intertwined
c) Dodie Clark
d) Composed

7 What star sign is Dodie?

a) Sagittarius
b) Aries
c) Taurus
d) Scorpio

8 Which UK city did Dodie live in with fellow YouTuber Jamie Jo?

a) Bath
b) Durham
c) London
d) Manchester

9 Which one of these is NOT the title of an original song by Dodie?

a) Courage
b) She
c) Rain
d) Fickle

10 Which date did Dodie Clark reach one million subscribers?

a) 4 July 2016
b) 25 December 2016
c) 11 April 2017
d) 3 May 2017

TRUE YOUTUBE FAN! ___ / 10

Turn to page **142** for the answers

109

CAN YOU GUESS THE YOUTUBER FROM THEIR BOOK QUOTE?

Nowadays there are so many YouTuber books out there, it's hard to keep track and read them all. But one thing is certain; the writing style of every book reflects its author pretty clearly. So, do you think you can match the YouTuber to a quote from their very own precious book?

Time to find out with this bookish quiz!

TRUE YOUTUBE FAN!

___ / 8

Turn to page **142** for the answers

1

'Every time you post something online you have a choice. You can either it something that adds to the happiness levels in the world – or you can m it something that takes away.'

a)   **Zoella**
b)   **Tyler Oakley**
c)   **PewDiePie**

2

'You have to make a change and walk away from the people who are bringing you down.'

a)   **Joey Graceffa**
b)   **KSI**
c)   **Marcus Butler**

3

'What do you call it when you drink prison hooch out of a coffee cup? A mug shot!'

a)   **Dan & Phil**
b)   **Hannah Hart**
c)   **Mamrie Hart**

4

'I looked up from my Scrabble letters and into his hazel eyes. Hazel is how you describe the color of someone's brown eyes when you're in love.'

a)   **Zoella**
b)   **Shane Dawson**
c)   **Tyler Oakley**

5

'But there's no need to be discouraged, you skin-covered meat puppet of potential.'

a)   **Dan & Phil**
b)   **Grace Helbig**
c)   **Marcus Butler**

6

'When the apocalypse comes, it won't just be cockroaches that survive. It will also be herpes and that random bottle of crème de menthe you bought years ago.'

a)   **Mamrie Hart**
b)   **Alfie Deyes**
c)   **Miranda Sings**

7

'THE DUCK IS COMING.'

a)   **KSI**
b)   **Mamrie Hart**
c)   **PewDiePie**

8

'How you get over a broken heart is to stop being sad. Easy. Or get revenge.'

a)   **Miranda Sings**
b)   **Tyler Oakley**
c)   **Alfie Deyes**

Can You Tell The Real YouTuber From The Photoshopped One?

Here are some pictures of some of your favourite YouTubers. Each has a side-by-side pic of the same photo – but one of the pictures has been very slightly edited. Your task is to work out which pic is the real deal and which is the unreal deal. Good luck!

AQ:

You spend an extra night doing the show, and it was fun; but you definitely feel like it's taking it out of you. Afterwards you can see people on Twitter saying you were acting a bit moody during the meet and greets...

- To reply to someone about it, turn to page 116
- To joke about it, turn to page 130

Turn to page **142** for the answers

TRUE YOUTUBE FAN! ___ / 8

1 PewDiePie

2 Anna Akana

3 Dodie Clark

4 AmazingPhil

5 Zoella

6 Caspar Lee

7 Markiplier

8 Joe Sugg

CAN YOU FIND ALL OF THE GAMERS IN THIS GAMING WORD SEARCH?

If you know your Let's Plays from your SSSniperwolf's and Minecraft from Markiplier then this word search should be pretty easy. There are 12 names of gaming creators hidden; time yourself and try and get them all in two minutes flat.

Turns out skipping the extra night was the right call – you forgot you have a sponsored video to make! But you forgot to bring the thing you have to promote on tour. What do you do?

- To make a video without the thing, turn to page 132
- To ask the sponsor to reschedule, turn to page 134

```
E  U  N  I  T  N  O  C  O  T  T  R  A  E  H  S  S  E  R
D  O  T  S  D  A  N  F  N  H  R  S  E  F  A  V  R  Q  P
J  D  L  H  K  I  I  H  A  S  C  U  P  Q  U  A  K  E  V  T
B  A  K  Z  A  Y  K  X  V  T  P  J  D  I  D  N  H  C  I  R
F  N  C  L  F  U  D  K  G  N  I  M  S  G  S  O  O  N  A  V
B  T  J  K  L  T  C  O  G  H  Z  I  E  N  O  S  Q  U  V  F
E  D  R  Q  S  S  C  Q  E  P  P  O  A  E  L  S  B  E  W  K
K  M  T  A  Q  E  I  J  A  S  I  J  N  R  K  G  Y  X  E  L
P  E  W  D  I  E  P  I  E  G  M  Y  A  E  Q  A  L  F  H  E
S  H  K  S  D  M  M  T  O  L  D  I  N  V  I  M  W  H  V  M
G  Z  F  T  Q  O  U  O  I  A  K  T  N  S  A  I  E  U  O  I
N  X  C  O  A  B  O  Y  L  C  X  H  E  E  M  N  Y  I  C  N
R  D  X  G  J  B  S  W  M  H  E  M  R  H  C  G  X  C  V  I
D  U  V  H  K  Q  O  X  H  W  Z  Y  S  R  B  R  Q  Q  S  M
T  E  I  E  Z  D  X  I  B  V  X  O  E  P  P  A  A  B  G  I
B  T  Q  Q  A  D  Q  N  H  K  M  E  D  O  T  O  E  F  F  N
W  R  I  H  Z  R  C  B  K  S  L  T  G  L  X  W  X  Q  T  T
R  Q  S  M  E  P  S  F  K  F  A  F  M  L  Z  C  C  M  C  E
F  D  P  V  C  K  W  E  B  B  L  E  K  O  P  C  P  U  A  R
L  T  N  R  T  O  R  S  D  I  E  Y  N  X  Q  A  D  F  E  S
```

1.	PewDiePie	7.	SeaNanners
2.	Kwebblekop	8.	iHasCupquake
3.	jacksepticeye	9.	LDShadowLady
4.	Vanossgaming	10.	DanTDM
5.	Smosh	11.	PressHeartToContinue
6.	miniminter	12.	Sky Does Minecraft

IS THIS JOE SUGG OR A TUGBOAT?

This is the true test of Joe Sugg fans. It took over 15 hours of Joe Sugg research to put together. It is perhaps the most in-depth Joe Sugg quiz ever created by man.

AQ:

Uh oh; you replied to someone on Twitter to clear things up – but now a lot of your really loyal fans are ganging up on this person! Time to try again before things get worse.

- To start over, turn to page 103
- To go back a step, turn to page 112/108

1

So you think you're a Joe Sugg fan? Well tell us this – is this a photo of Joe Sugg?

a) **That's Joe Sugg**
b) **That's a tugboat**

2

And what about this picture?

a) **That's definitely Joe Sugg.**
b) **That's a tugboat, I swear it.**

3

Who is this though?

a) **That's Joe Sugg and a pug.**
b) **What? You think I'm a fool? That's clearly a tugboat.**

4

We think this is one of Joe's best pics, don't you agree?

a) **Yeah he looks great!**
b) **Nice try – that's a tugboat.**

5

Who is this?

a) **That's a Suggboat.**
b) **That's a tugboat.**

6

What about this?

a) **That's a pugboat and it's majestic.**
b) **That's Joe Sugg.**

TRUE
YOUTUBE
FAN!

___ / 6

Turn to page **142** for the answers

ARE THESE ZOELLA FACTS TRUE 👍 OR 👎 FALSE?

Zoella continues to go from strength to strength and has an incredible 11 million+ subscribers. Perhaps you're one of Zoë's millions of fans but how well do you really know the YouTube fave? This quiz is all about which facts are true and which are false.

AQ: What were you thinking? Real people spent their real money to see you! Now everyone online is mad – even people who weren't going. Your reputation is ruined. Come on – you had to know this one was a dead end, right?

- To start over, turn to page 103
- To go back a step, turn to page 132

1 Zoë's middle name is Elizabeth.

True ☐ False ☐

2 Zoë is an Aries.

True ☐ False ☐

3 As a child, Zoë lived in Singapore for two years.

True ☐ False ☐

4 Zoë had a cat named Ginger when she was growing up.

True ☐ False ☐

5 Zoë is 5 foot 5.

True ☐ False ☐

6 Zoë's favourite food is M&Ms.

True ☐ False ☐

7 The Aristocats is Zoë's favourite Disney movie.

True ☐ False ☐

8 Zoë used to work in New Look.

True ☐ False ☐

9 Zoë won the 2012 Cosmopolitan award for Best Beauty Vlogger.

True ☐ False ☐

10 Zoë once said she had a phobia of the colour red.

True ☐ False ☐

TRUE YOUTUBE FAN!

___ / 10

Turn to page **142** for the answers

HOW MANY YOUTUBER BOOKS HAVE YOU READ?

As you'll note from this quiz, hardly any* YouTubers have taken the opportunity to sign a book deal and none of them have ever click-baited a video with news of a predictable special announcement. It's time to own up and confess your shame. How many of these YouTuber books do you actually own? Double points if you've read them past the first two chapters.

*EVERY. SINGLE. ONE.

AQ: The power nap on the train wasn't the most comfy – but it was worth it! You felt more refreshed than before and smashed your show. Congrats!

- To start over, turn to page 103

- [ ] 1. Arden Rose, *Almost Adulting*
- [ ] 2. Alfie Deyes, *The Scrapbook of my Life*
- [ ] 3. Alfie Deyes, *The Pointless Book*
- [ ] 4. Alfie Deyes, *The Pointless Book 2*
- [ ] 5. Bethany Mota, *Make Your Mind Up*
- [ ] 6. Carrie Hope Fletcher, *All I Know Now*
- [ ] 7. Caspar Lee, *Caspar Lee*
- [ ] 8. Charlie McDonnell, *Fun Science*
- [ ] 9. Connie Glynn, *The Rosewood Chronicles*
- [ ] 10. Connor Franta, *A Work In Progress*
- [ ] 11. Connor Franta, *Note To Self*
- [ ] 12. Dan Howell and Phil Lester, *Dan And Phil Go Outside*
- [ ] 13. Dan Howell and Phil Lester, *The Amazing Book Is Not On Fire*
- [ ] 14. Emma Blackery, *Feel Good 101*
- [ ] 15. Estée Lalonde, *Bloom*
- [ ] 16. Eva Gutowski, *The Struggle Is Real*
- [ ] 17. Fleur DeForce, *The Glam Guide*
- [ ] 18. Fleur DeForce, *The Luxe Life*
- [ ] 19. Grace Helbig, *Grace and Style*
- [ ] 20. Grace Helbig, *Grace's Guide: The Art of Pretending to Be a Grown Up*
- [ ] 21. Grace Victory, *No Filter*
- [ ] 22. Hannah Hart, *Buffering*
- [ ] 23. Hannah Hart, *My Drunk Kitchen*
- [ ] 24. Hannah Witton, *Doing It!*
- [ ] 25. iJustine, *I, Justine: An Analog Memoir*
- [ ] 26. Jim Chapman, *147 Things*
- [ ] 27. Joe Sugg, *Username: Evie*
- [ ] 28. Joe Sugg, *Username: Regenerated*
- [ ] 29. Joey Graceffa, *Children of Eden*
- [ ] 30. Joey Graceffa, *In Real Life*
- [ ] 31. John Green, *Paper Towns*
- [ ] 32. John Green, *The Fa...*
- [ ] 33. KSI, *I Am A Bellend*
- [ ] 34. Lilly Singh, *How To Be A...*
- [ ] 35. Louise Pentland, *Life With... of Glitter*
- [ ] 36. Louise Pentland, *Wilde Like M...*
- [ ] 37. Mamrie Hart, *You Deserve A Drin...*
- [ ] 38. Marcus Butler, *Hello Life!*
- [ ] 39. Marzia Bisognin, *Dream House*
- [ ] 40. Melanie Murphy, *Fully Functioning Human (Almost)*
- [ ] 41. Michelle Phan, *Make Up: Your Life Guide to Beauty, Style, and Success*
- [ ] 42. Miranda Sings, *Selp-Helf*
- [ ] 43. Niomi Smart, *Eat Smart*
- [ ] 44. Oli White, *Generation Next*
- [ ] 45. Oli White, *The Takeover*
- [ ] 46. PewDiePie, *This Book Loves You*
- [ ] 47. Ricky Dillon, *Follow Me*
- [ ] 48. Rosanna Pansino, *The Nerdy Nummies Cookbook*
- [ ] 49. Ryan Higa, *How to Write Good*
- [ ] 50. Savannah Brown, *Graffiti*
- [ ] 51. Shane Dawson, *I Hate Myselfie*
- [ ] 52. Shane Dawson, *It Gets Worse*
- [ ] 53. Sidemen, *Sidemen: The Book*
- [ ] 54. Tanya Burr, *Love, Tanya*
- [ ] 55. Tanya Burr, *Tanya Bakes*
- [ ] 56. Thomas Ridgewell, *Art Is Dead: The Asdf Book*
- [ ] 57. Tyler Oakley, *Binge*
- [ ] 58. We The Unicorns, *World of Youtube*
- [ ] 59. We The Unicorns, *Vlogging 101*
- [ ] 60. Will Darbyshire, *This Modern Love*
- [ ] 61. Zoë Sugg, *Girl Online*
- [ ] 62. Zoë Sugg, *Girl Online: Going Solo*
- [ ] 63. Zoë Sugg, *Girl Online: On Tour*

TOTAL: ___ /63

Score: 0-20: Somehow, you've resisted the temptation to fill your shelves with every single book. However, we'll have you know that you are seriously missing out on some literary greats and even Shakespeare himself would want you to read Generation Next by Oli White. / 21-40: With a mix of YouTubers, legit authors and the odd coffee table book in your collection, you've got your taste down to a tee. You feel like you have to but you will go out there and support your favourite creators. Just promise us our books are your favourite, OK? / 41-60+: Do you know how many trees sacrificed themselves for your collection of YouTuber books, huh? Why not clear out the not-so-good from the good and donate some to charity?

ONLY REAL SIDEMEN FANS WILL GET 100% ON THIS QUIZ

The Sidemen are easily one of the biggest, most popular YouTube squads on the Internet – but how much do you know about KSI, miniminter, Zerkaa, TBJZL, Behzinga, Vikkstar123 and Wroetoshow?

From the date they formed to the order each member joined, this quiz is the only way to prove with 100% accuracy that you're the biggest fan in the whole world – time to prove you're ultimate enough for this squad.

AQ:

You wake up to frantic pounding on the door of your hotel room – you've slept in and missed your train! Tonight's show is going to be delayed by nearly an hour. Well done, rockstar...

- To start over, turn to page 103
- To go back a step, turn to page 132/130/136

How many official members of the Sidemen are there?
a)   7
b)   8
c)   9

 What was the group originally called?
a)   Extreme Sidemen
b)   Ultimate Sidemen
c)   Quintessential Sidemen

 What year in school did KSI and Simon Minter meet?
a)   Year 6
b)   Year 7
c)   Year 8

 How would Simon help KSI's channel back in the day?
a)   He edited his videos
b)   He held the camera
c)   He played him in FIFA

 Who was officially the third member of the group?
a)   Zerkaa
b)   Vikkstar123
c)   TBJZL

 When did the Ultimate Sidemen officially form?
a)   19 October 2013
b)   20 October 2013
c)   20 October 2014

 Which TV channel hos~ their show, The Sideme. Experience?
a)   MTV
b)   BBC Three
c)   Comedy Central

 What is this their main game of choice?
a)   Grand Theft Auto
b)   FIFA
c)   Call of Duty

 Where did they play their charity football match in June 2016?
a)   Southampton
b)   Birmingham
c)   Bournemouth

 What was the final score of their charity football match against the YouTube Allstars (YTAS)?
a)   SDMN 2 - 7 YTAS
b)   SDMN 5 - 3 YTAS
c)   SDMN 7 - 2 YTAS

 What Sidemen event happened for the first time on the 12 November 2016?
a)   Download
b)   Upload
c)   Refresh

 Which one of these members does not live in the official Sidemen house?
a)   KSI
b)   Josh
c)   Ethan

Turn to page 142 for the answers

___ / 12

TRUE YOUTUBE FAN!

Match The YouTuber To Their

Confession

YouTuber's have a LOT of secrets. Whether they're revealing their favourite kind of peanut butter, or the fact that they've not been wearing a bra all day, there's a special art to matching the shocking confession to the red-faced YouTuber. Here are eight mysterious and very revealing YouTuber confessions from Twitter, and all you need to do is figure out who the dastardly deed belongs to.

AQ:

You write a post, and a lot more of the response becomes more understanding and positive. You're feeling excited about the rest of the tour; so it's time to make a video.

- To film an update about the whole thing, turn to page 130
- To go live on Instagram, turn to page 136

1. 'I have a confession to make. Up until about a year ago...I would put pineapple on pizza. I hope you can find it in your heart to forgive me.'

🗨 🔁 ♡ ✉

----
a)   Caspar Lee
b)   Phillip DeFranco
c)   Ethan Klein

2. 'Confession: I've never had a spa day. Or even a spa treatment. Contemplating visiting one? Are they actually fun? Or boring?

🗨 🔁 ♡ ✉

----
a)   Manny Mua
b)   Tanya Burr
c)   Em Ford

3. 'Confession: it took me like 6 months to figure out that "IRL" meant "in real life". I thought it was some new version of a URL.'

🗨 🔁 ♡ ✉

----
a)   Colleen Ballinger
b)   Miranda Sings
c)   Grace Helbig

4. 'Confession: I really can't handle beach holidays as not doing stuff makes me really under stimulated and sad.'

🗨 🔁 ♡ ✉

----
a)   Lucy Moon
b)   Zoella
c)   Anna Saccone-Joly

5. 'Lil YouTube confe... every creator is co... channel is dying and... isn't good enough.'

🗨 🔁 ♡

----
a)   Emma Pickles
b)   Evan Edinger
c)   Dodie Clark

6. 'Confession – I have a crush on @Zoella'

🗨 🔁 ♡ ✉

----
a)   Colleen Ballinger
b)   Alfie Deyes
c)   Caspar Lee

7. 'You guys I have a confession: I never did the ice bucket challenge.'

🗨 🔁 ♡ ✉

----
a)   KSI
b)   Christine Sydelko
c)   Luke Cutforth

8. 'I have a confession to make... I only take npc's in video games because I think they might give me things.'

🗨 🔁 ♡ ✉

----
a)   KickThePj
b)   jacksepticeye
c)   CrankGamePlays

TRUE YOUTUBE FAN! _____ / 8

Turn to page **142** for the answers

THE MOST EPIC, ULTIMATE, ABSOLUTELY INCREDIBLY WONDERFULLY HARD YOUTUBE TRIVIA QUIZ IN A BOOK FULL OF YOUTUBE QUIZZES!

TRUE YOUTUBE FAN!

As you may have guessed from the title, this quiz is the absolute be all and end all when it comes to YouTuber quizzes. This quiz is going to throw up some serious YouTube history and school the hell out of you. From couples to birthdays, viral videos to beauty products, there's extra points to be won so be sure to prove your worth!

1 What are the names of the three YouTube founders?

a) Theo, Michael, Daniel
b) Hollie, Benedict, Liam
c) Jawed, Chad, Steve

2 What was Mark Ferris' original channel name?

a) TheBiffLovesYou
b) YTKilledTheRadioStar
c) MonsterMunch45

3 What are the first names of Zoë and Joe Sugg's parents?
One point for each name.

a) Gary
b) Harry
c) Graham

a) Tracey
b) Christine
c) Elaine

4 Which one of these viral videos was released in 2010?

a) Shoes
b) Old Spice advert
c) Leave Britney Alone

5 How old was Rebecca Black when she released the iconic track 'Friday'?

a) 13
b) 14
c) 16

6 Speaking of Rebecca Black, give yourself TWO points if you know her middle name?

a) Bridget
b) Celine
c) Renee

7 Who was the first UK creator to receive one million subscribers?

a) Charlie McDonnell
b) Zoë Sugg
c) KickThePj

8 Which star's music video proved so popular that it broke YouTube's view count? (Seriously, it had far too many for YouTube to deal with. And we bet a LOT of them came from you!).

a) OKGO
b) Psy
c) Taylor Swift

MORE QUESTIONS
THIS WAY

Which YouTuber is known for curling her hair with a whole lot of weird stuff including Cheetos and fidget spinners?

a) **grav3yardgirl**
b) **Inthefrow**
c) **Ingrid Nilsen**

Which one of these YouTubers was a professional cricketer at one point?

a) **PewDiePie**
b) **Ryan Higa**
c) **Josh Pieters**

Which clothing brand did Bethany Mota release a range with?

a) **River Island**
b) **Aeropostale**
c) **Jack Wills**

A chance for DOUBLE POINTS!
We've listed eight names below but which two are the names of Gabriella Lindley's cats?

a) **Fluffy**
b) **Jeremy**
c) **Bert**
d) **Luna**
e) **Gordon**
f) **Lana**
g) **Nellie**
h) **Ariana**

What month was PewDiePie born in?

a) **May**
b) **October**
c) **December**

Who doesn't love a YouTuber wedding? And Tanya Burr and Jim Chapman's was one of the most iconic to date... but when did the pair wed?

a) **25 June 2014**
b) **3 September 2015**
c) **3 May 2016**

It's one of the most well-known viral videos ever but what year was 'Chocolate Rain' released?

a) **2007**
b) **2010**
c) **2011**

16 For FOUR points, circle the names of the Chapman siblings...

a) Jim
b) John
c) Nic
d) Jo
e) Hannah
f) Sam
g) Robin
h) Stephanie
i) Tanya

17 In Jake Paul's stunning musical debut, where does Nick Crompton claim he is not from?

a) Sunderland
b) Boston
c) Compton

18 Which brand did Jaclyn Hill collaborate with to release a range of poppin' highlighters and face products?

a) Becca
b) Too Faced
c) Rimmel

19 How many subscribers does a channel need to get the silver play button?

a) 50,000
b) 100,000
c) 250,000

20 What date did JennaMarbles reach one million subscribers on YouTube?

a) 2 September 2010
b) 4 September 2011
c) 9 September 2012

Turn to page **142** for the answers

___ / **26**

BUILD A COLLAB VIDEO AND WE'LL GIVE YOU AN (IDEAL) YOUTUBER

Coming up with the perfect collab video is hard. Not only do you need a fun new idea; but you also need to pick the perfect buddy to feature in your video. Luckily, with our extensive YouTube knowledge, it's entirely possible to figure out your dream collab partner. All you need is the perfect video idea. So with this carefully-crafted quiz, you can finally get the answers you're looking for.

People appreciate that you can make light of it; you're only human after all! But still, you could really use a break before tonight's show...

- To have a lie-in, turn to page 122
- To try and sleep on your train, turn to page 120

1 What type of video are you making?

a) Challenge
b) Discussion
c) Reaction
d) Sketch
e) Q&A
f) How To
g) Music
h) No idea

2 Where are you filming?

a) In an office
b) At work
c) In a bedroom
d) In a studio
e) Out in the world
f) On set
g) In your house
h) In nature

3 How many YouTubers would be in your ideal collab?

a, d & e) As many as can fit onscreen

b, c & f) Just the one

g & h) About 2–3 people

4 Will there be alcohol involved?

a, f, g & h) Hell yeah drink up

b, c, d & e) Heck no I'm a child of the Lord

5 How about any awkwardness?

a, c, e & g) Well, if it gets the clicks...

b, d, f & h) Big nah!

6 Pick a collab video c

a) Video starts wi out-take
b) Never making eye contact
c) Laughter sounds fake
d) An extra YouTuber crashes the video
e) It's a #spon video
f) An unexpected pet guest
g) Too much awkwardness
h) Someone is blindfolded

7 What would you do for a 'punishment'?

a) Electric shocks
b) Something bad-tasting
c) Free slaps
d) Eat or drink something foul
e) Whipped cream in the face
f) Take a shot
g) Down your drink
h) Homemade gunge

8 Lastly, pick someone you WOULDN'T collab with...

a) iDubbbz
b) Matthew Santoro
c) Tana Mongeau
d) Tanya Burr
e) TomSka
f) Hannah Witton
g) Liza Koshy
h) Jack Howard

Mostly As: Tyler Oakley / Mostly Bs: Ash Hardell / Mostly Cs: Dan Howell / Mostly Ds: Lilly Singh / Mostly Es: Caspar Lee / Mostly Fs: Hannah Hart / Mostly Gs: Jon Cozart / Mostly Hs: Miranda Sings

COULD YOU ACTUALLY SURVIVE WITHOUT YOUTUBE?

So, you're thinking one of two things about your ability to survive without YouTube:

1. You'd be absolutely banging at living in a world without the joy and creativity of YouTubers

or

2. Life would slowly become hell on earth until you eventually realised that you simply could not exist without vloggers

So take this quiz and figure out the path your life will take once YouTube is inevitably sucked into the vacuous and empty realm of space. Yes, this is where YouTube will realistically end up. And, if it's gonna happen in the next seven years as we predict, you need to prepare yourself as to whether or not you'd survive the cut.

AQ:

For some reason the brand loves your creative decision of making the video without the product — that was lucky! But now you're pretty exhausted from touring and video-making...

- To have a lie-in, turn to page 122
- To say "YOLO" and cancel a show, turn to page 118

Okay, think about your favourite YouTuber... do they upload on a daily basis?

a) **Yes, like clockwork**
b) **Nope, it's totally irregular**
c) **They post once, maybe twice a week**
d) **When they post they go social media crazy so I always find it**
e) **I don't watch it straight away so don't know**

What is the first thing you do when you wake up?

a) **Check my subscriptions**
b) **Check my emails**
c) **Check my Snapchat**
d) **Go to the toilet**
e) **Roll over and go back to sleep**

Have you been to a YouTube convention before?

a) **Yes! About 10 million**
b) **I accidentally met a YouTuber in the streets, but never at a convention**
c) **Nah mate, can't afford it**
d) **I'm going to my first one this year**
e) **I might go to one... I've not decided yet TBH**

Have you ever dreamt of being a YouTuber before?

a) **Dreamt?! I AM ONE!**
b) **Yeah ofc, but I'll never do it**
c) **I made a video once, but it was tragic**
d) **Yeah for sure**
e) **No way, I'd be terrible**

Are you the 'G◼◼◼ Expert' in your fr◼◼

a) **For sure, I'm a◼**
b) **I know a couple◼ but I'm not an exp◼**
c) **I'm good, but I'm n◼ THAT good**
d) **I'm like, 97% sure I co◼ win a YouTube IQ fight**
e) **Nah, I'm an expert on REAL world things like socks and grapes**

And finally, you need to choose between these two deadly serious options:

a & b) You can ONLY watch halfway through every single YouTube video henceforth

c, d & e) You can ONLY watch videos with under 500,000 views for the rest of time

Mostly As: Absolutely not. You'd be dead in a week. / Mostly Bs: You'd stand a pretty good chance of surviving... but will eventually sell your soul for just one more 'Primark Haul' video. / Mostly Cs: Actually, you'd be totally fine. You'd spend every night crying for no reason, but you'd survive at least! / Mostly Ds: After months without YouTube, you eventually crack and start trying to film your cat cleaning itself. It's one way to help with your withdrawal symptoms, but it's definitely not what some people call 'surviving'. / Mostly Es: Meh, no YouTube is easy for you. Which we totally don't understand.

WHO'S THAT YOUTUBER?

Can you catch 'em all? See if you can find and recognise these YouTubers in the wild, using just their silhouettes to guide you.

AQ:

Oh no! Because you can't deliver on time the sponsor is dropping the project. Better not tell anybody you're the reason this brand won't work with YouTubers anymore...

- To start over, turn to page 103
- To go back a step, turn to page 114

ALFIE DEYES
AMAZINGPHIL
CASPAR LEE
DAN HOWELL
JOE SUGG

MIRANDA SING.
PEWDIEPIE
TYLER OAKLEY
ZOELLA

1.

2.

3.

4.

5.

6.

7.

8.

9.

Turn to page **142** for the answers

___ / 9

TRUE
YOUTUBE
FAN!

The True YouTube Fan Score Sheet

It's time for the moment of truth. Once you've completed every single quiz in this book you'll not only have come to a better understanding of yourself and your place in this universe, but you'll also be able to calculate your True YouTube Fan score. Write in your score for each quiz listed, and then add them up (you can use your phone, this isn't a maths test) to find out your whether you're a True YouTube Fan.

AQ: Oh, that wasn't smart. Somebody watching the livestream figured out which hotel you're staying in, and now swarms of fans are waiting outside! How do you respond?

- To do a late-night impromptu meet-up, turn to page 122
- To Tweet telling them to go away, turn to page 106

TOTAL: _____

Turn the page to find out whether you're a true YouTube fan...

Are You A True YouTube Fan?

Between 0 and 79
Just in case you don't know, YouTube is an amazing website where you can watch videos from some very talented creators. You might like it. Check it out, and then try completing this book again.

Between 80 and 179
You did OK, but we certainly wouldn't call you a True Fan. Brush up on your YouTube knowledge by reading more We The Unicorns books, or check out wetheunicorns.com – those guys know what they're talking 'bout.

Between 180 and 250
You like YouTube a lot, that's clear, but there are some gaps in your knowledge. You've probably learnt some new facts and picked up some interesting tips on new creators to watch.
You're welcome.

Between 251 and 337
You've done it; you've proven yourself a True YouTube Fan. There's nothing about YouTube that you don't know that's worth knowing.

338+
Your score is utterly perfect. You can do no better – if you did, check your maths! All shall bow to your superior YouTube knowledge. You're more than a True YouTube Fan; in fact you may be some kind of all-knowing, all video-seeing entity.

ANSWERS - Oi! No Cheati

Pages 4–7: We Regret To Inform You That This Quiz Is Indeed, The Harde

1. Maybelline / **2.** Jack Harries / **3.** Rapidash / **4.** Vanessa Hudgens / **5.** Ryar ToysReview / **6.** Connor Franta / **7.** Fleur DeForce / **8.** Michael / **9.** Zoë Sugg / **10.** Pakistan / **11.** Cosmopolitan / **12.** Suki / **13.** Psychology / **14.** 'All of Me' by John Legend / **15.** JennaMarbles

Pages 8–9: Match The YouTuber To Their Middle Name

1. Dodie Miranda Clark / **2.** Jenna Nicole Marbles / **3.** Philip James DeFranco / **4.** Connor Joel Franta / **5.** Phil Michael Lester / **6.** Colleen Mae Ballinger / **7.** Zoë Elizabeth Sugg / **8.** Ian Andrew Hecox / **9.** Felix Arvid Ulf Kjellberg

Pages 14–15: Name The YouTuber From The Picture Clues

1. jacksepticeye / **2.** Markiplier / **3.** Dan Howell (danisnotonfire) / **4.** AmazingPhil / **5.** Lilly Singh / **6.** Nathan Zed

Pages 18–19: Can You Tell If These Facts Are True Or False?

1. No real / **2.** No real – Benefit was not one of the counters she worked on. / **3.** Real – his sister Zoë did appear as an extra in the films however. / **4.** Real / **5.** Real / **6.** No real – it's Elizabeth. / **7.** No real / **8.** No real – she's actually called Cheryl. / **9.** Real / **10.** No real – he had a hamster named Suki.

Pages 20–22: How Well Do You Remember The Lyrics To Dan's Diss Track?

1. A tag / **2.** By his fringe / **3.** 2007 / **4.** Slenderman / **5.** Being judged is scary / **6.** Eating / **7.** Three weeks / **8.** It's kawaii / **9.** Toast / **10.** Evan Peters / **11.** Furry / **12.** Ryan Higa

Pages 28–29: Unscramble These YouTuber Names In The Ultimate Anagram Quiz

1. Zoella / **2.** jacksepticeye / **3.** Dodie Clark / **4.** Phil Lester / **5.** Alfie Deyes / **6.** Tyler Oakley / **7.** Lilly Singh / **8.** Markiplier / **9.** Shane Dawson / **10.** Liza Koshy / **11.** Ryan Higa / **12.** Jacksfilms / **13.** Saccone Jolys / **14.** Daniel Howell

Pages 30–31: Match The YouTuber To The Trend They Invented

1. Louise Pentland / **2.** Ryan Higa / **3.** Filthy Frank / **4.** Phil Lester / **5.** KeepingUpWithXK / **6.** Simply Nailogical

·33: Test Your Parents' YouTube Knowledge
...on the left / **2.** Zoella / **3.** Over a billion / **4.** PewDiePie / **5.** A YouTube
...tion / **6.** Joe (Sugg) / **7.** Irish (jacksepticeye)

·s 34–35: Is This Connor Franta Or A Can Of Fanta?
...onnor Franta / **2.** That's a can of Fanta / **3.** Connor Fanta / **4.** The great city
...Atlanta / **5.** A noble manta / **6.** A can of Franta

Pages 36–37: Can You Guess The YouTuber From Their Birthday?
1. Gabriella Lindley / **2.** Bethany Mota / **3.** Tyler Oakley / **4.** Tana Mongaeu /
5. DanTDM / **6.** Oli White / **7.** Samantha Chapman

Pages 42–43: The Hardest NikkieTutorials Quiz Ever
1. Pisces / **2.** The Netherlands / **3.** 2008 / **4.** The Hills / **5.** Her mother / **6.** 6 feet
2 inches / **7.** Amsterdam / **8.** The Power Of Makeup

Pages 50–51: Match The YouTuber To Their Instagram Post
1. Liza Koshy / **2.** Gabriella Lindley / **3.** Chanel Ambrose / **4.** Laci Green /
5. Zoë Sugg / **6.** Dodie Clark / **7.** Phil Lester / **8.** Nathan Zed / **9.** Connor Franta

Pages 52–53: Who Are We Talking About?
1. Fleur DeForce / **2.** Jack Maynard / **3.** Bethany Mota / **4.** Emma Blackery /
5. Thomas Sanders / **6.** Captain Sparklez / **7.** GloZell / **8.** Jacob Sartorius /
9. Rose and Rosie / **10.** Samantha Maria / **11.** Miranda Sings / **12.** Gigi Gorgeous

Pages 54–55: Can You Match The YouTuber To Their Comments?
1. Dan Howell / **2.** Lilly Singh / **3.** Dodie Clark / **4.** Nathan Zed / **5.** Gabriella /
6. Humza Productions / **7.** Zoella / **8.** Mark Ferris / **9.** Hannah Hart

Pages 58–59: Can You Match The Revelmode Icon To The YouTuber?
1. KickThePj / **2.** Dodger / **3.** Cryaotic / **4.** CinnamonToastKen / **5.** CutiePieMarzia /
6. Jelly / **7.** Emma Blackery / **8.** PewDiePie / **9.** Slogoman

Pages 64–65: Is This The Name Of A Video Game Or YouTube Channel?
1. Video Game / **2.** YouTube Channel / **3.** YouTube Channel / **4.** Video Game /
5. YouTube Channel / **6.** Video Game / **7.** YouTube Channel / **8.** Video Game /
9. Video Game / **10.** YouTube Channel

Pages 66–67: How Many Gaming YouTubers Can You Find In This Word Search?
CaptainSparklez / jacksepticeye / IHasCupQuake / Smosh Games / Markiplier /
Stampylonghead / VanossGaming / PopularMMOS / SSSniperwolf / PewDiePie /
LDShadowLady / SeaNanners / Yogscast – did you find any more?

Pages 68–69: Match The YouTuber To Their Book Title
1. Marcus Butler / **2.** Zoë Sugg / **3.** Miranda Sings / **4.** Tyler Oakley / McDonnell / **6.** Connor Franta / **7.** Oli White / **8.** Dan and Phil / **9.** Beth

Pages 70-71: Who Is Older? Celebrities Vs YouTubers
1. Dan Howell / **2.** Charlie Puth / **3.** Taylor Swift / **4.** Miles McKenna / **5.** Cris Ronaldo / **6.** Hilary Duff / **7.** Hannah Witton / **8.** Grace Victory / **9.** Niall Hora **10.** Lele Pons

Pages 72–73: Match These YouTubers To Their Hometowns
1. Wayne Goss > Burnham-on-Sea / **2.** Louise Pentland > Northampton / **3.** Hannah Witton > Manchester / **4.** KSI > Watford / **5.** Jamie Genevieve > Glasgow / **6.** Joe Sugg > Lacock / **7.** Phil Lester > Rawtenstall / **8.** Gabriella Lindley > Sheffield / **9.** Emma Blackery > Basildon / **10.** Jim Chapman > Norwich / **11.** Jonathan Joly > Dublin / **12.** Samantha Maria > Harrow

Pages 74–75: Can You Guess The YouTuber We've Pixelated?
1. Dodie Clark / **2.** Shane Dawson / **3.** Zoë Sugg / **4.** Joey Graceffa / **5.** Tana Mongeau / **6.** Elijah Daniel / **7.** Scola Dondo / **8.** iHasCupquake / **9.** Caspar Lee

Pages 78–79: JennaMarbles True Or False
1. True / **2.** False / **3.** False / **4.** True / **5.** False / **6.** True / **7.** True / **8.** False / **9.** False / **10.** False

Pages 80–81: Match The YouTuber To Their Surname
1. Haste / **2.** Zelalem / **3.** Ridgewell / **4.** Magrath / **5.** Coburn / **6.** Fuentes / **7.** McLoughlin / **8.** Fischbach / **9.** Connell / **10.** Sopher / **11.** Porteous / **12.** Gardner

Pages 86–87: How Well Do You Know The Lyrics To 'Friday'?
1. Fresh / **2.** Bus stop / **3.** Seat / **4.** Highway / **5.** Fun / **6.** Kickin' / **7.** Ball / **8.** Weekend / **9.** Friday

Pages 94–95: Odd One Out
1. charlieissocoollike / **2.** Phil Lester / **3.** Joe Sugg / **4.** Shane Dawson / **5.** JennaMarbles / **6.** Kingsley / **7.** Tyler Oakley / **8.** grav3yardgirl / **9.** Jamie's World / **10.** The Phandom, obviously

Pages 96–97: Match the YouTuber To Their Song Lyric
1. Miranda Sings / **2.** Tay Zonday / **3.** Joey Graceffa / **4.** Jon Cozart / **5.** Dodie Clark / **6.** Marcus Butler / **7.** Julia Nunes / **8.** The Midnight Beast / **9.** Tessa Violet

Pages 104–105: Can You Match The YouTuber To Their Nickname?
1. Gabriella Lindley / **2.** Joe Sugg / **3.** Connor Franta / **4.** Dan Howell / **5.** GloZell Green / **6.** Tyler Oakley / **7.** Carrie Hope Fletcher / **8.** Louise Pentland / **9.** PJ Liguori

y / 2. 2017 / **3.** Joshua / **4.** Saxophone / **5.** Jon Cozart / **6.** Intertwined /
/ 8. Bath / **9.** Courage / **10.** 11 April 2017

es 110–111: Can You Guess The YouTuber From Their Book Quote?
oella / 2. Marcus Butler / **3.** Hannah Hart / **4.** Tyler Oakley / **5.** Grace Helbig /
. Mamrie Hart / **7.** PewDiePie / **8.** Miranda Sings

Pages 112–113: Can You Tell The Real YouTuber From The Photoshopped One?
1. The left image is real / **2.** The right image is real / **3.** The right image is real /
4. The left image is real / **5.** The right image is real / **6.** The left image is real /
7. The right image is real / **8.** The left image is real

Pages 116–117: Is This Joe Sugg Or A Tugboat?
1. Joe Sugg / **2.** Tugboat / **3.** Joe Sugg and a pug / **4.** Tugboat / **5.** Suggboat /
6. Pugboat

Pages 118–119: Are These Zoella Facts True Or False?
1. True / **2.** True / **3.** False / **4.** False / **5.** False / **6.** False / **7.** False / **8.** True /
9. True / **10.** False

Pages 122–123: Only Real Sidemen Fans Will Get 100% On This Quiz
1. 7 / **2.** Ultimate Sidemen / **3.** Year 8 / **4.** He held the camera / **5.** Zerkaa /
6. 19 October 2013 / **7.** Comedy Central / **8.** FIFA / **9.** Southampton / **10.** SDMN
7 - 2 YTAS / **11.** Upload / **12.** Ethan

Pages 124–125: Match The YouTuber To Their Confession
1. Phillip DeFranco / **2.** Em Ford / **3.** Colleen Ballinger / **4.** Lucy Moon /
5. Dodie Clark / **6.** Colleen Ballinger / **7.** Christine Sydelko / **8.** KickThePj

Pages 126–129: The Most Epic, Ultimate, Absolutely Incredibly Wonderfully Hard YouTube Trivia Quiz In A Book Full Of YouTube Quizzes!
1. Jawed, Chad, Steve / **2.** TheBiffLovesYou / **3.** Graham and Tracey / **4.** Old
Spice advert / **5.** 13 / **6.** Renee / **7.** Charlie McDonnell / **8.** Psy / **9.** grav3yardgirl /
10. Josh Pieters / **11.** Aeropostale / **12.** Jeremy and Nellie / **13.** October /
14. 3 September 2015 / **15.** 2007 / **16.** Jim, John, Nic and Sam / **17.** Compton /
18. Becca / **19.** 100,000 / **20.** 4 September 2011

Pages 134–135: Who's That YouTuber?
1. AmazingPhil / **2.** Caspar Lee / **3.** Dan Howell / **4.** Joe Sugg / **5.** Miranda Sings /
6. PewDiePie / **7.** Alfie Deyes / **8.** Zoella / **9.** Tyler Oakley

Picture Credits

Interiors

Studio Press and **wetheunicorns.com** would like to thank the following people: Michaela Walters, Megan Wastell, Stone Wilson-Beales, Hollie Brooks, Liam Dryden, Benedict Townsend, Charley Hodson, Fiona Morris and Frances Prior-Reeves.

ALSO AVAILABLE

WORLD OF YOUTUBE

YOUTUBE YEARBOOK